THE
GOSPEL
FOR LIFE

SERIES

THE GOSPEL &

Religious
Liberty

THE
GOSPEL
FOR LIFE

—— SERIES ——

THE GOSPEL &

Religious
Liberty

SERIES EDITORS

RUSSELL MOORE *and*
ANDREW T. WALKER

NASHVILLE, TENNESSEE

978-1-4336-9047-1

Published by B&H Publishing Group
Nashville, Tennessee

Dewey Decimal Classification: 261.72
Subject Heading: GOSPEL \ FREEDOM OF RELIGION \
CHRISTIANITY AND POLITICS

All Scripture is taken from the Holy Bible, English
Standard Version, copyright © 2001 by Crossway Bibles,
a publishing ministry of Good News Publishers.

1 2 3 4 5 6 7 8 • 21 20 19 18 17 16

CONTENTS

Series Preface

Russell Moore

Why Should *The Gospel for Life* Series Matter to Churches?

IN ACTS CHAPTER 2, WE READ ABOUT THE DAY OF PENTECOST, the day when the resurrected Lord Jesus sent the Holy Spirit. The Day of Pentecost was a spectacular day—there were manifestations of fire, languages being spoken by people who didn't know them, and thousands of unbelievers coming to faith in this recently resurrected Messiah. Reading this passage, we go from account to account of heavenly shock and awe, and yet the passage ends in an unexpectedly simple way: "And they devoted themselves to the apostles' teaching and the fellowship, to the breaking of bread and the prayers" (Acts 2:42).

I believe one thing the Holy Spirit wants us to understand from this is that these "ordinary" things are not less miraculous than what preceded them—in fact, they may be more so. The disciplines of discipleship, fellowship, community, and prayer are the signs that tell us the kingdom of Christ is here. That means that for Christians, the most crucial moments in our walk with Jesus Christ don't happen in the thrill of "spiritual highs." They happen in the common hum of everyday life in quiet, faithful obedience to Christ.

That's what *The Gospel for Life* series is about: taking the truths of Scripture, the story of our redemption and adoption by a risen Lord Jesus, and applying them to the questions and situations that we all face in the ordinary course of life.

Our hope is that churches will not merely find these books interesting, but also helpful. *The Gospel for Life* series is meant to assist pastors and church leaders to answer urgent questions that people are asking, questions that the church isn't always immediately ready to answer. Whether in a counseling session or alongside a sermon series, these books are intended to come alongside church leaders in discipling members to see their lives with a Kingdom mentality.

Believers don't live the Christian life in isolation but rather as part of a gospel community, the church. That's why we have structured *The Gospel for Life* series to be easily utilized in anything from a small group study context to a new member or new believer class. None of us can live worthy of the gospel by ourselves and, thankfully, none have to.

Why are we so preoccupied with the idea of living life by and through the gospel? The answer is actually quite simple: because the gospel changes everything. The gospel isn't a mere theological system or a political idea, though it shapes both our theology and our politics. The gospel is the Good News that there is a Kingdom far above and beyond the borders of this world, where death is dead and sin and sorrow cease. The gospel is about how God brings this Kingdom to us by reconciling us to Himself through Christ.

That means two things. First, it means the gospel fulfills the hopes that our idols have promised and betrayed. The Scripture says that all God's promises are yes in Jesus (2 Cor. 1:20). As sinful human beings, we all tend to think what we really want is freedom from authority, inheritance without obedience like the prodigal son. But what Jesus offers is the authority we were designed to live under, an inheritance we by no means deserve to share, and the freedom that truly satisfies our souls.

Second, this means that the gospel isn't just the start of the Christian life but rather the vehicle that carries it along. The gospel is about the daily reality of living as an adopted child of a resurrected Father-King, whose Kingdom is here and is still coming. By looking at our jobs, our marriages, our families, our government, and the entire universe through a gospel lens, we live differently. We will work and marry and vote with a Kingdom mind-set, one that prioritizes the permanent things of

Christ above the fleeting pleasures of sin and the vaporous things of this world.

The Gospel for Life series is about helping Christians and churches navigate life in the Kingdom while we wait for the return of its King and its ultimate consummation. The stakes are high. To get the gospel wrong when it comes to marriage can lead to a generation's worth of confusion about what marriage even is. To get the gospel wrong on adoption can leave millions of "unwanted" children at the mercy of ruthless sex traffickers and callous abusers. There's no safe space in the universe where getting the gospel wrong will be merely an academic blunder. That's why these books exist—to help you and your church understand what the gospel is and what it means for life.

Theology doesn't just think; it walks, weeps, and bleeds. *The Gospel for Life* series is a resource intended to help Christians see their theology do just that. When you see all of life from the perspective of the Kingdom, everything changes. It's not just about miraculous moments or intense religious experiences. Our gospel is indeed miraculous, but as the disciples in Acts learned, it's also a gospel of the ordinary.

Introduction

Andrew T. Walker

RELIGIOUS LIBERTY IS AMONG THE MOST IMPORTANT AND most misunderstood topics today in America. You may have heard of this phrase "religious liberty" and were unaware of just how fundamental it is to our faith as Christians, but also to the list of rights we hold as fundamental in America.

As many know from their childhood education, those who came to America and who helped found this country did so fleeing religious persecution in their native country. It isn't an accident, therefore, that religious liberty is listed in the First Amendment to the United States Constitution. Why is this? Why did the founders of our country lay this principle at the very foundation of a new country?

Because to be free to believe, and free to live out those beliefs, is the very cornerstone of a free society. Religious liberty is the right that secures and anchors all other rights. How so? Religious liberty arises from the truth that a person's relationship with God is the most important relationship a person can have. It's so important that no law or state should be able to interfere with a person's relationship to God or his or her ability to live out his or her faith.

In the same way, religious liberty teaches that religious truth cannot be coerced. Because it cannot be coerced, religion ought to be freely pursued.

Some opponents of religious liberty characterize "religious liberty" as a code word for bigotry. They warn that religious liberty is really a disguise for anti-gay, anti-liberal, or anti-progressive political policies. The accusation comes, ironically, from interest groups who claim to advocate for civil liberties, albeit at the expense of liberty itself. Nothing could be further from the truth. The perspective of this book is neither Left nor Right; liberal nor conservative. Instead, we believe we can have meaningful discourse about religious liberty, free of any conspiracy to promote a particular political viewpoint. Simply put: Religious liberty benefits liberals, conservatives, Democrats, Republicans, Christians, and non-Christians alike. Religious liberty is a virtue for the common good. Religious liberty and conscience lie at the foundation that allows difference to flourish!

Christians should have particular care for religious liberty because it's the pillar that allows the church to fulfill its mission. Religious liberty means we have the freedom to pledge allegiance to a power greater than the state itself.

Additionally, we ought to care for religious liberty out of love for our neighbor. As we see around the world, the countries most hostile to liberty and freedom are the same countries that take aim to stamp out religious liberty. For the sake of our own worship, and the dignity and freedom of others—who we disagree with about God—we ought to be a people that looks to maximize and protect this most cherished doctrine, religious liberty.

As American culture loses its attachment to its Christian roots, and as Christianity grows stranger and stranger in what it teaches and upholds as beautiful, Christians will need to be able to articulate why religious liberty matters not just to Christians, but to all people who desire to live in a free society. We see this happening already when journalists place scare quotes around "religious liberty" as though religious liberty is merely a pseudonym for discrimination. As a country, we've tragically moved away from religious liberty being a bipartisan issue to now being seen as a partisan issue—most often in the context of sexual ethics.

Each book in *The Gospel for Life* series is structured the same: What are we for? What does the gospel say? How should the Christian live? How should the church engage? What does the culture say?

The Gospel & Religious Liberty is intended to be an introductory look at how religious liberty applies to every angle of the Christian's life—their place in culture, their engagement as everyday Christians, and their role in the body of Christ—the church. We want no stone unturned when talking about how the gospel of Jesus Christ and its impact on religious liberty shapes us as a people on mission.

We hope that as you come away from this volume, you'll have a better understanding of why religious liberty matters so crucially not just to Christians, but also to all persons. Religious liberty can often be an abstract concept, so we've worked hard in this volume to make understanding religious liberty as accessible as possible in hopes that all Christians will be better informed about standing up for religious liberty.

We hope you'll see from the Bible why God desires His creatures to worship Him freely. We hope you'll see why your voice as a citizen and your participating in a local church intersects so greatly with protecting religious liberty.

CHAPTER

1

What Are We For?

Andrew T. Walker

NOWHERE IN THE BIBLE DOES IT SAY THAT 2 + 2 = 4.

But if you're like me, you've been taught that the Bible is the highest authority that informs our understanding of the Christian faith and shapes how we see the world. So, if there isn't a verse that says 2 + 2 = 4, does that mean it's still true?

The answer is a simple "yes," because God created all minds to understand logical truths. It isn't just Christians that understand that 2 + 2 = 4; it's a simple fact of our existence. If you're sitting and reading this chapter, it means that God put your mind together with the capacity to read and make sense of letters and words. In a way, Psalm 24:1 speaks to these truths: "The earth is the LORD's and the fullness thereof, the world and those who dwell therein."

Everything—whether knowledge, mathematics, or the enjoyment of a hot fudge sundae—exists because it exists in God's world and God holds the world together (Gen. 1; Col. 1).

Why does this matter in talking about what the Bible says about religious liberty?

From this little thought exercise, we learn an important truth that will help guide our discussion about religious liberty; namely, that there are *explicit* truths of Scripture and *implicit* truths of Scripture. Some things are very clearly declared in Scripture; for example, Jesus is God's Son. But nowhere does the Bible talk about humans breathing oxygen or that 2 + 2 = 4, yet we'd all affirm that the importance of breathing oxygen is implied in how God chose to create humanity and that the truths of mathematics makes sense because God is the author of logic.

We, therefore, understand religious liberty as an *implied* truth of Scripture, one we see throughout, though not explicitly stated.

There isn't a verse in the Bible that says, "Thou shalt have religious liberty." Jesus didn't commission His disciples to announce, "Repent, for the dawning of religious liberty has come." Yet, many themes that we draw from the Bible imply that religious liberty is a bedrock value that is central to so much of the Bible's narrative about God, salvation, mission, and even government. And when you look at the narrative of Scripture and what realities the Scriptures are pointing us to, religious liberty and the commitment to free expression are central to God's story.

In this chapter, we're going to look at a few biblical truths and explain why religious liberty is a common thread that helps make sense of so many biblical themes, and why valuing religious liberty is an expression of loving one's neighbor and a main ingredient for a free society. Many of the themes below overlap with one another, which helps us to see how central religious liberty is to the Bible overall.

God and Religious Liberty

In the Ten Commandments, God commands the Israelites in Exodus 20:3 saying, "You shall have no other gods before me."

Why does this matter to religious liberty? Because God is teaching that nothing should set itself up as a god that isn't YHWH the God of Israel. Because God is ultimate, it is wrong when things set themselves up as gods that aren't God. When Genesis 1:1 says that God *created*, it implies that only God is sovereign. It didn't say, for example, that the United States *created*. Religious liberty begins with God as the primary Creator and Author of Life.

Whenever a movement, a figure, or a government attempts to play the part of God, it acts grievously wrong. Creations cannot and should not play the role of a Creator. Nothing should set itself up as ultimate that isn't ultimate.

It especially means that institutions, movements, persons, or governments shouldn't act to determine truths in areas that don't belong to them. For example, it wouldn't be right for my daughter's teacher to tell my daughter to disobey what my wife and I have instructed her. A teacher doesn't have ultimate authority over my daughter in the ways that my wife and I do. In the same way, a government shouldn't tell a citizen who God is or how God wants to be worshipped. It is therefore right and good for persons, governments, or institutions to restrict themselves to the area that they're designed to have authority over. A government is designed to see that laws are followed and that citizens are protected. The government isn't designed to tell you or me what the meaning of baptism is.

Now, this is kind of complex, but this understanding of religious liberty played a very important part in how the United States understood religious liberty at its founding.

James Madison, one of the architects of our Constitution said it this way:

> It is the duty of every man to render to the Creator such homage and such only as he believes to be acceptable to him. This duty is precedent, both in order of time and in degree of obligation, to the claims of Civil Society. Before any man can be

considered as a member of Civil Society, he must
be considered as a subject of the Governour of the
Universe: And if a member of Civil Society, who
enters into any subordinate Association, must always
do it with a reservation of his duty to the General
Authority; much more must every man who becomes
a member of any particular Civil Society, do it with a
saving of his allegiance to the Universal Sovereign.[1]

What Madison argues is what the Bible is implicitly shouting from its very first verse. Madison argues that a person's relationship to God is prior to any other relationship that a person has. How a person understands what is true, good, and beautiful are such transcendent truths that the government has no rightful authority to dictate its citizens' opinions on such matters. Religious liberty is not an absolute right; nor are society or government just blank slates. Religious liberty doesn't lead to relativism. Religious liberty entails the careful balancing of a state's right to uphold public order and the rights of citizens to freely exercise their religion in peaceful ways.

What does this mean practically? It means that the state should not set itself up as lord or god over the conscience—that government employees shouldn't be intercessors and that judges shouldn't be the priests. When the state honors the First Amendment; that is, when it provides for the free exercise of religion, it is less likely to betray or violate the First

Commandment—which demands that we have no other gods other than God the Father of Jesus Christ.

The issue before us—the biblical issue—is one of authority and allegiances. To whom does our conscience belong? To God or the state? If the state can tell you what is or isn't acceptable belief about matters relating to God and ultimate morality, what can't it do?

In Acts, we read about the early church and their insistence that another King—King Jesus—reigns more supreme than Caesar.

According to Acts 17:6–7,

> And when they could not find them, they dragged
> Jason and some of the brothers before the city
> authorities, shouting, "These men who have turned
> the world upside down have come here also, and
> Jason has received them, and they are all acting
> against the decrees of Caesar, saying that there is
> another king, Jesus."

When the church announces that Jesus is Lord, a claim is being made that trumps all other claims that any king, Caesar, or president may make. The announcement that Jesus is Lord subjects other authorities to the highest authority.

Religious Liberty and Human Dignity

In Genesis 1:26–27, God announces something unique about His creation of humanity—that *only* humans would resemble or image God. Something is precious and unique to humanity that is unlike other parts of creation. Being created in the image of God means that every human being—born and unborn—is created with dignity and worth. Every human, on the basis of being alive, is deserving of certain rights and respect.

> Then God said, "Let us make man in our image,
> after our likeness. And let them have dominion over
> the fish of the sea and over the birds of the heavens
> and over the livestock and over all the earth and over
> every creeping thing that creeps on the earth."
> So God created man in his own image, in the
> image of God he created him; male and female he
> created them.

This matters to religious liberty because every person, whether Christian or not, cannot be coerced into the kingdom of God. While we may disagree with who a person understands God to be, every person has the right to seek God for himself or herself. The rights of individuals to seek and understand who God is—even when they perceive wrongly—is something that can only be determined between a person and who they perceive God as. Each person, as an image bearer, is created with a conscience; and Christians should respect the consciences of those who come to a different opinion about who God is.

This is not to say that all quests to find God are equal. Unless someone professes Jesus Christ as Lord and Savior, Christians must insist that all quests are in vain and lead to separation from the one true God (Acts 4:12).

But neither you nor I can understand who God is for someone else. We can converse, contend, plead, and work to persuade every living person that the only God is the triune God, but because every person is made in the image of God, they should have the right to discern who God is without other persons or government infringing on that quest.

To allow a person to live out what he or she considers to be ultimate truth is to allow a person to live with integrity. John Henry Newman famously wrote, "Conscience has rights because it has duties."[2]

The conscience—religiously anchored or not—in how it understands and perceives its relationship with ultimate reality and transcendent truth, must be unhindered, according to Henry. Why? *Because to prevent an individual from fulfilling or acting on what they believe is their highest responsibility, highest obligation, or their most supreme understanding of truth is to rob them of their freedom and their dignity.* As image bearers of God, we all possess rational faculties that drive us to live out these truths and obligations.

To seek after God, as Notre Dame sociologist Christian Smith has framed it, is what makes us "believing animals."[3] To rob someone of their freedom to exercise his or her religion is to deny a very fundamental aspect of their personhood. Indeed, to deny or strip someone his or her religious freedom individually or on a social level is to disrupt the natural rhythms of a nation or society whose citizens find their moral bearings from religion.

In sum, you ought to be able to "love the Lord your God with all your heart and with all your soul and with all your mind and with all your strength" freely and without interference (Mark 12:30).

We don't have to like that others claim religious truth aside from the Bible. We don't have to like that other religions contend for adherents. But we cannot coerce people's minds away from what they perceive as true. What must occur is the art of persuasion and evangelism—not forcing someone to agree with us.

Government and Religious Liberty

The role of government has been touched upon only briefly throughout this chapter so far. How government understands religious diversity in its midst is one of the most important considerations a government can make. A country and civilization's freedom often hinge upon whether its government allows for genuine religious diversity to flourish. Indeed, a survey of countries today shows that those governments most opposed to religious diversity are the same government's most opposed to individual liberty. Religious liberty and individual liberty go hand in hand because a state that doesn't restrict personal liberty is also likely to allow religious liberty to flourish.

A very important passage about God and government is Romans 13:1–7.

> Let every person be subject to the governing authorities. For there is no authority except from God, and those that exist have been instituted by God. Therefore whoever resists the authorities resists what God has appointed, and those who resist will incur judgment. For rulers are not a terror to good conduct, but to bad. Would you have no fear of the one who is in authority? Then do what is good, and you will receive his approval, for he is God's servant for your good. But if you do wrong, be afraid, for he does not bear the sword in vain. For he is the servant of God, an avenger who carries out God's wrath on the wrongdoer. Therefore one must be in subjection, not only to avoid God's wrath but also for the sake of conscience. For because of this you also pay taxes, for the authorities are ministers of God, attending to this very thing. Pay to all what is owed to them: taxes to whom taxes are owed, revenue to whom revenue

is owed, respect to whom respect is owed, honor to whom honor is owed.

What Paul teaches in Romans 13 is that, again, government's role is limited and its authority delegated. The Holy Spirit speaking through Paul doesn't say that the state is empowered to interfere in every sphere of a person's life. Rather, the ideal government is one that operates in its proper jurisdiction—administering law and protecting citizens—and doesn't attempt to absolutize its claims over every area of a person's life.

The principle that some things legitimately fall to government's accountability implies that there are areas of our existence that are not accountable to government. This principle is taught in Matthew 22:15–22. According to this passage,

> Then the Pharisees went and plotted how to entangle him in his words. And they sent their disciples to him, along with the Herodians, saying, "Teacher, we know that you are true and teach the way of God truthfully, and you do not care about anyone's opinion, for you are not swayed by appearances. Tell us, then, what you think. Is it lawful to pay taxes to Caesar, or not?" But Jesus, aware of their malice, said, "Why put me to the test, you hypocrites? Show me the coin for the tax." And they brought him a denarius. And Jesus said to them, "Whose likeness

and inscription is this?" They said, "Caesar's." Then
he said to them, "Therefore render to Caesar the
things that are Caesar's, and to God the things that
are God's." When they heard it, they marveled. And
they left him and went away.

In trying to trick Jesus into whom He pledged ultimate
authority to, Jesus craftily answered the Pharisees by insist-
ing that there are legitimate interests where His followers are
accountable to the state—such as taxation. But then Jesus notes
that Caesar and any other government doesn't have the right to
claim total authority. Like this chapter has stressed thus far, one
of those spheres where the government is not competent in is
matters of religion and theological truth claims.

This is really, really important. States mingling with religion
has a terrible track record. Where a state totally discards religion
by abolishing it, such atrocities like communism arose which
resulted in tyranny. With state churches that confuse citizenship in the state with membership in the kingdom of God, you
get dead churches and unregenerate Christians. When the state
treats religion with hostility, it props itself up as a false god.
When the state treats religion as an appendage to be controlled,
over time, it numbs and deadens religion once the state meddles
in Christian identity and Christian conscience—something that
Jesus never gave to it in Matthew 16:19.

The most biblical form of government is one that gets out of the way.

The most biblical form of government is one that's neither hostile to religion nor too cozy with religion.

The most biblical form of government is a government that allows Christian mission to prosper and compete against all other religions that equally seek to vie for acceptance.

The most biblical form of government is one that doesn't see itself as a totalizing or absolute force, but recognizes its limit and allows for religion to prosper freely and to compete in the marketplace of ideas.

As James Madison said, "The Religion then of every man must be left to the conviction and conscience of every man." It is an "arrogant pretension" to believe that "the Civil Magistrate is a competent Judge of Religious Truth."[4]

A Free Society and Religious Liberty

Jesus said, "You shall love your neighbor as yourself" (Mark 12:31). This simple truth implies a fundamental truth to living together in a diverse world: we should treat others the way we want to be treated. Think about how this applies very tangibly. If I don't want my religious beliefs targeted for harassment by the government, I shouldn't want the religious beliefs of other religions targeted either. I don't want my religious beliefs targeted by the government.

Since I don't want my rights to act on the deepest truths of my faith to be restricted simply because they're unpopular or perceived as strange by some, so I should be willing to extend this same courtesy to my neighbor who believes differently than I. A government that can impede on someone else's religion is a government that can impede on my religion.

A part of loving my neighbor is respecting their rights to pursue ultimate truth, as they perceive it.

Some may read that and object, saying, "Are you arguing for relativism? Are you saying anything goes and that whatever falls under the rubric of religion is untouchable? Are you saying, for example, that child sacrifice is okay if it is done under the protection of religious liberty?"

No, that's not what I'm saying. Where a religion's desire for free exercise legitimately harms the common good, such as public health, it is fair and reasonable for the government to restrict someone's religious liberty. And there are laws in place—such as the Religious Freedom Restoration Act—that help weigh a religion's free exercise against the government's claim that a religion is doing actual harm.

The principle at stake here is very important. A few years back, there was enormous blowback against plans to build a mosque at the location where the September 11, 2001, attacks occurred. Many individuals felt it insensitive to build a mosque on the grounds where a particularly violent strand of Islam carried out the attacks. While I understand the concerns about appropriateness and sensitivity, if law and cultural opinion can work to prevent Muslims from obtaining legal permits to construct a mosque (something the First Amendment protects), law and cultural opinion can act just as easily to prevent a church to be built if and when law and culture deem the church's beliefs unpopular and, therefore, unwelcome. In difficult instances like these, we should defer to liberty for the sake of protecting the interests of others and our own.

In 1 Corinthians 10:31, the apostle Paul states that "whether you eat or drink, or whatever you do, do all to the glory of God." Aside from the implications for God's glory, the assumption in this text is that all obstacles should be removed from our path in order to advance God's glory. Thus, where a person is unable to live out their religious commitment, they are not only robbing themselves of living faithfully, they are robbing God of His glory.

In a very well-known case involving Hobby Lobby, the owners believed that God's glory was at stake in the government's mandate that Hobby Lobby provide its employees with insurance coverage that included access to pills that could potentially cause an abortion. When Hobby Lobby sued the government, the owners didn't do so for political reasons. They did so because they believed the government was impeding its ability to live out the owners' values through how they ran their business. Thankfully, the Supreme Court sided with Hobby Lobby.

Finally, in Matthew 19:16–22, we learn the lesson of the rich young ruler.

> And behold, a man came up to him, saying, "Teacher, what good deed must I do to have eternal life?" And he said to him, "Why do you ask me about what is good? There is only one who is good. If you would enter life, keep the commandments." He said to him, "Which ones?" And Jesus said, "You shall not murder, You shall not commit adultery, You shall not steal, You shall not bear false witness, Honor your father and mother, and, You shall love your neighbor as yourself." The young man said to him, "All these I have kept. What do I still lack?" Jesus said to him, "If you would be perfect, go, sell what you possess and give to the poor, and you will have treasure in heaven; and come, follow me." When the young man heard this he went away sorrowful, for he had great possessions.

What do we observe here? Hidden in the text is something very, very important. Jesus did not coerce the rich young ruler to follow Him. The man was given the choice of whether to follow

Jesus. While making the wrong decision, the man's wishes to reject Jesus were respected.

If Christians are to defend religious liberty, we must do so on the grounds that no person can be argued or forced into the kingdom of God.

Mission and Religious Liberty

Jesus' call to the Great Commission has implications for religious liberty, perhaps most of all. According to Matthew, before Jesus ascended into heaven, He gave His disciples these instructions:

> Now the eleven disciples went to Galilee, to the mountain to which Jesus had directed them. And when they saw him they worshiped him, but some doubted. And Jesus came and said to them, "All authority in heaven and on earth has been given to me. Go therefore and make disciples of all nations, baptizing them in the name of the Father and of the Son and of the Holy Spirit, teaching them to observe all that I have commanded you. And behold, I am with you always, to the end of the age." (Matt. 28:16–20)

Jesus' instructions are to take the gospel to every corner of the world. For the gospel to advance, it needs a pathway. That's religious liberty. Religious liberty assures that Christians possess the freedom and safety to live out and advance the cause of Christ.

The Great Commission is where the points of this chapter all culminate, as all things should.

We advance religious liberty because the glory of God is at stake.

We advance religious liberty because we believe that every person is created in God's image and accountable to Him and where God has placed him (Acts 17:25–26).

We advance religious liberty because a nation that protects religious diversity is a nation that respects its citizens.

We advance religious liberty because a nation that understands that its laws and commands are not ultimate makes for a government that doesn't try to play the role of God.

We advance religious liberty because to uphold our own freedoms to proclaim the glory of God in Christ requires that other religions have the ability to live and proclaim their beliefs freely, too.

Religious liberty isn't simply an abstract concept that we believe in because the Constitution of the United States upholds it (though that is very important). We believe religious liberty is vital to the advance of the gospel. To be sure, regardless of whatever government Christians find themselves, the gospel will advance. This is happening even now in Asia where regimes hostile to the gospel cannot stop its advance, despite every effort. Using our God-given rights to appeal for religious liberty's advance is a righteous cause motivated by our desire to see as many people come to Christ as possible (Acts 25).

When Christians protect and advance religious liberty not only for ourselves but also for all, we protect the free market of ideas that allows the gospel to be ushered into every corner of culture. The purpose of religious liberty, ultimately, is to advance the cause of the gospel so that God's glory may advance.

Discussion Questions

1. Why does the Bible's command that we not worship false gods have importance for religious liberty?
2. Have you been made to participate in something that you objected to or didn't agree with? Did being forced to participate in something make you enjoy that which you were participating in? If not, why then should Christians fight for the religious liberty of all people?
3. Why is religious liberty so central to the Great Commission?

CHAPTER

2

What Does the Gospel Say?

Russell Moore

And as [Paul] was saying these things in his defense, Festus said with a loud voice, "Paul, you are out of your mind; your great learning is driving you out of your mind." But Paul said, "I am not out of my mind, most excellent Festus, but I am speaking true and rational words. For the king knows about these things, and to him I speak boldly. For I am persuaded that none of these things has escaped his notice, for this has not been done in a corner. King Agrippa, do

you believe the prophets? I know that you believe."
And Agrippa said to Paul, "In a short time would
you persuade me to be a Christian?" And Paul said,
"Whether short or long, I would to God that not
only you but also all who hear me this day might
become such as I am—except for these chains." Then
the king rose, and the governor, and Bernice, and
those where were sitting with them. And when they
had withdrawn, they said to one another, "This man
is doing nothing to deserve death or imprisonment."
And Agrippa said to Festus, "This man could have
been set free if he had not appealed to Caesar." (Acts
26:24–32)

ON A SUMMER DAY IN BILOXI, MISSISSIPPI, I WAS ALMOST
kicked out of the Cub Scouts.

In those days I and my fellow Scouts were trying to earn the
God and Country merit badge. Part of the requirement for the
badge was visiting a local church and meeting its pastor. For us,
this meant sitting down with a Methodist pastor to talk about
what it meant to be good Christians, what it meant to be good
Americans, and what it meant to be good citizens. I remember
that he talked a lot about morality and clean living. He talked
about being free and being Americans and being good. Finally he
concluded: "Any questions you have for me as a pastor?"

And I, a little boy from Woolmarket Baptist Church, raised my hand and said, "Some people say that a Christian can be possessed by a demon, and some people say that a Christian can't be possessed by a demon. What do you think?" I'll never forget his answer: "I don't believe in demons."

I was horrified. My twelve-year-old mind couldn't believe that such a man could be pastor of a Methodist church. Immediately sensing the call to take up Jesus' whip in the temple, I took out my Bible and started showing him all the verses that referred to demons. At last he said, "I know all of that but I don't believe the Bible is talking about things that are really true. I think these are metaphors that simply tell us how we ought to live in this life." This little Southern Baptist kid with a solid twelve years' worth of theological knowledge fired back immediately: "But that's not Christianity."

My Scout leader did his best to calm me down and end the debate with the preacher. But I just kept thinking if all this is just about making us good moral citizens, then it doesn't't line up with everything that I've learned about the gospel of Jesus Christ. Even if my pre-teenage vocabulary couldn't express this, even then I knew I felt it in my soul: If what matters most is getting us to behave, then we will not be meriting God and country, but hell.

Why has this memory stayed with me all these years? Because it was the moment I first confronted the "almost-gospel" of generic, mush civil religion, the kind that talks about morality but doesn't talk about Christ. My encounter with the well-meaning Methodist pastor alerted me to the fact that there is a decaffeinated Christianity that simply affirms whatever the outside culture sees as good and virtuous and useful. It is precisely this pseudo-Christianity with which the outside culture has never had and will never have a problem.

It is the Christianity that is authentic, bold, and real that Jesus tells us is what starts cosmic warfare. The light goes into the darkness and the darkness revolts against the light. And that is precisely the kind of world that our churches, our pastors, our seminaries, and our children are now living in. Nominal Christianity is collapsing at its core.

The Conflict of a Gospel Witness

Why? The reasons are many, but the fundamental cause is this: Our surrounding culture has become secularized to the point that being known as a Christian or belonging to a Christian church are not symbols of respectability. Being identified as a Christian is no longer a pathway to favor—it isn't useful. Nominal Christianity cannot survive the loss of social respectability because nominal Christianity is custom-designed to foster social respectability. So yes, generic, social Christianity is collapsing, but the good news is that it leaves something in its place. As nominal Christianity disappears, what remains is a vibrant, gospel-focused, cross-preaching, evangelizing book-of-Acts Christianity. It's this authentic Christian faith that looks so strange, ridiculous, and even repugnant in American culture.

That means conflict. It means the same kind of conflict that every age of the church of Jesus Christ has experienced. In recent years we've had all sorts of debates about whether Christians will be raptured before the tribulation or after it, but at the same time nominal Christians are being raptured by the culture itself. Forget the Great Tribulation; nominal Christians are being raptured right now by the secular culture. They are increasingly moving away from the church. Sometimes Christians have been upset about this. But the disappearance of cultural Christianity should not cause Christians to bemoan what they've lost, but rather to embrace the opportunity to proclaim authentic Christianity, knowing that wherever the gospel is proclaimed opposition will present itself. That's what the fight for religious liberty in every single era of the church is about.

That's why we have to realize that the right for religious liberty is given to the entire church. Pastors, elders, teachers, and counselors of Jesus' congregations have a spiritual obligation to shape consciences that know how to stand up and assert the freedom of the church in a free state.

We have a model for this, and his name is Paul.

Paul writes repeatedly that the aim of his ministry and service is to help those who will come after him. We see Paul all through the book of Acts and throughout his epistles constantly at odds with the authorities over his freedom to preach, disciple, evangelize, plant churches, and carry forward the gospel. As we watch Paul's life unfold in Scripture, one thing in particular stands out—the way he balances the centrality of the gospel with the prioritization of religious liberty. How did he do it? Fortunately, the Scriptures tell us how.

In Acts 26 we see that Paul has landed himself in trouble, because the gospel he is preaching is creating tensions that are so strong riots are breaking out in the temple. People are saying he is a troublemaker who is subverting the will of the Roman Empire. He makes waves in every culture he steps into. What we see from this passage is that Paul goes to tremendous personal pains, all the way to the chambers of the most powerful people in Rome, to maintain his freedom to do this.

The question is: Why? Paul is speaking in his own defense before Agrippa. He is defending himself against those who are saying that he has no right to preach this gospel. Not only that, but the fact that people are threatened by Paul's message is a sign that they really understand it. An unclear message isn't threatening. Paul is emulating what Jesus and the other apostles have consistently modeled: whenever they are being well received, they clarify the message even further.

Think of how counterintuitive this seems to our notion of how to win over a crowd. The Lord's disciples thought so too. They were constantly irritated with Jesus because every time that it seems as though they are making progress—people gathering up by the thousands, eating miraculously provided loaves and fishes and ready to hear a sermon—the Messiah stands up before a Jewish audience and says something like, "Unless you eat My flesh and drink My blood, you can have no life in you." The people primed to give Jesus their "vote" hear Him (seemingly) upend the laws they've heard from childhood about touching dead bodies or eating something with blood. The disciples probably couldn't understand it at first. When someone asked Jesus, "What must I do to inherit eternal life," Jesus continued to press and make absolutely sure they understood how scandalous His claims are. He clarified the nature of the gospel and the nature of Christianity until it created a crisis, whether in the individual or in the society.

Paul has learned well from Jesus. Paul knew if he had simply come into Athens or Corinth or Ephesus and preached a bland sort of spirituality and nothing more, he would have been well received. But that's not what happens. Instead, Paul preaches repentance, faith, Jesus Christ, the resurrection, and the exclusivity of Christ. The result: The silversmiths are offended because their business is in jeopardy. The philosophers are offended because their philosophy is in jeopardy. Those who want to hold on to their immorality are offended because their sexual freedom is challenged. Even still, Paul stands his ground and speaks in his own defense.

Maybe that sounds strange to us. After all, this is the same guy who says elsewhere, "I have thrown everything away for the sake of the gospel. I count nothing of my own privilege as being important except for the gospel." We know Paul. We know he would willingly go to jail, make tents for a living, endure shipwreck and abandonment and brutal public beatings. We know Paul is a man who did not stand and claim privileges for himself. But here he is standing in court and defending himself. Why? Because Paul understands that his liberty to preach the gospel is itself a gospel issue. If the Roman Empire is able to assert its lordship over the conscience, the empire has become a god. When Paul says to the government, "I am going to appeal all the way up the chain here in my own defense," he knows he's not looking for a favor from Uncle Nero. He's advocating on behalf of divine right of the gospel.

We're Not the Empire's Chaplains

There's an important lesson in this for all of us. When Christians say to their government that they must live freely and exercise their beliefs freely and that everybody else in the country ought to exercise their beliefs and their consciences freely, they're not asking for a favor from the government. The church isn't a business in need of a bailout. Rather, the church is just asserting what is true. On the Day of Judgment, when the hearts of all mankind are weighed, the United States Congress will not be sitting on the judges' panel. Human government has no jurisdiction over the souls of mankind. By using all of his resources to appeal all the way to the top of the Roman hierarchy, Paul is sending a message, and it's a message that is certainly not about him. Telling the empire, "No, you cannot limit my soul freedom," is about the advance of the gospel. Religious liberty isn't about Paul, and it's not about us. It is about the Word that came out of the Greco-Roman Empire all the way down through human history for millennia to wherever it was that you first heard it preached. In defending himself, Paul isn't puffing himself up; he is pouring himself out.

This is precisely the same task that the church in every single generation has faced and will face. Fast-forward from Paul in the Roman Empire to our evangelical chaplains in the United States military in the twenty-first century. These Christians are faced every single day with exactly these same questions and choices. They're told, "We want you to pray, but we want you to pray in ways that are generic and non-sectarian. Don't pray in Jesus' name; just say, 'We pray in Your name.' You'll know who you are talking about and God will know who you are talking about, but you won't offend and you won't disrupt other people." And immediately the temptation is to fold. Immediately this confessional Christian chaplain is reasoning: "Well, in order for me to carry out my ministry, I'm just going to do what they are telling me to do." But the problem is exactly about "ministry." The government of Paul's day and the government of this chaplain's day are trying to set up something generic, something entirely different. Governments have legitimate authority over all sorts of areas, but prayer isn't one of them. The proper response from a godly, courageous chaplain is to insist, "Sir, when I am praying, I'm not talking to you, sir." He, like Paul before him, is defending not only his own freedom but the religious liberty of all of those who will come later.

Returning to Paul's example before the Romans, we see Paul remaining steadfast on both the reasonableness and the strangeness of the gospel. As he is defending himself, Festus tells Paul he is out of his mind. I remember as a seminary student feeling like this had happened to me. In moments of mental exhaustion I was sure I had studied too much and wasn't capable of thinking clearly anymore. Festus thinks that is what happened to Paul. He has been shut up in his room with his books for so long that he's gone crazy. Paul's reply is simple. He says, "No, I'm speaking to you true and rational words. These are things that you've seen in the prophets. These are things that have happened in the world you live in, not in my mind or my bookshelf." Paul is in his right mind.

Learning to Disagree and Persuade

Now some Christians look at this and other moments in Scripture and they feel brave and bold. They read and then they think, *Yes, that's exactly why people don't take me seriously! They hated Elijah and John the Baptist and they just hate me too because I speak the truth!* Well, that could be true, but it could also be the case that they're a jerk. The world is indeed lost and wrong about God, but that doesn't mean the world is always wrong about us. Sometimes people think a Christian is crazy because that particular Christian is actually acting like it.

But of course, that's not what is happening with Paul. Paul is speaking a word of persuasion. He is speaking in rational and reasonable words and making a defense. He is taking his listeners seriously and his choice of words reflects that. Paul understands something that contemporary Christians often don't. Before someone will listen to a preacher preach about the gospel, they need to know that person actually cares about them. Credibility follows empathy. No Christian or church or "community outreach project" should expect unbelieving culture to take it seriously if the feeling is not reciprocated. A message can be as bold and courageous and powerful as you like, but if it is tailored to get "Amens" from the people who already agree with it, it's not prophetic ministry.

Paul is speaking to people who fundamentally disagree with him. Actually, they think he's insane. Instead of throwing his hands up and looking for an easier audience, Paul goes to work. He knows why they believe what he is saying is crazy, so he goes about this strategically. His first step is finding the point of agreement: "I am being accused by the Jews because of this hope. Why is it considered incredible by any of you that God raises the dead?" Paul is talking to them on their terms. He invites them to consider and evaluate his message rationally. Paul knows his message is reasonable, and he wants these unbelievers to see that.

But Paul doesn't stop there. He knows Christianity isn't just a reasonable message. It's a strange one too. When I was in seminary I served as a youth minister, and one aspect of that ministry I found particularly difficult was trying to evangelize teenagers who knew how to talk about Christianity but didn't actually know Christ. The stories of the Bible were something they'd seamlessly absorbed growing up, just like saying, "Yes, ma'am," and "No, ma'am." They were totally untroubled by the gospel.

But there was another group of kids at our church, many of whom were fatherless and had never been in a church building before. They lived at the Air Force base down the street and would come into church sometimes cloaked with a thick scent of marijuana. They had no concept of Christianity or the message of the Bible. One student would raise his hands and interject: "Now, wait a minute, so you really believe that this dead guy came back to life?" I told him I did. "You really believe the dead guy came back to life, he's still alive, and he's gonna come back in the sky?" I said yes. His conclusion? "Dude, that is crazy."

No Christian should be surprised at this exchange. The claims of the gospel are not tame; they are extraordinary and supernatural. One of the most counterproductive ways to defend religious liberty is to make Christianity seem normal. Far too many American Christians have envisioned Christianity to be everything you already want *plus* heaven at the end. That's not the formula for the gospel of Jesus Christ. In fact, the only place that kind of Christianity sells is a nominal Christian culture. It's not compatible with a culture of Christians who worship and love and submit to a resurrected Warrior-King. There's a reason that most best-selling "prosperity gospel" books don't get translated into Sudanese. If you might be crucified for your allegiance to the Lord Jesus, it's difficult to see the connection between God's favor and a new Mercedes.

Paul certainly didn't grieve the "weirdness" of his Christian message. Actually, he did the opposite of grieve; he pressed his advantage and put the demands of the gospel in the face of his audience. It's not enough for Paul to get a hearing. He wants faith. He wants repentance and conversion. This isn't merely a moment for Paul's religious liberty. It's a moment for the people listening to him. Agreeing with Paul about his right to preach the gospel isn't sufficient, because the gospel requires a response.

Paul is not settling for external morality. That's because Paul knows nominal Christianity might be comfortable with Christian ethics, but it is not comfortable with Christ. The "how" of religious liberty is certainly important, but the "why" is infinitely more so. The freedom that we petition for is not a freedom to preserve our traditions or our comfort. It's a freedom to be relentless in pressing the gospel call for everyone everywhere. That's what Paul did. He didn't waste his freedom. Whether he was in a Philippian jail, getting beaten by a mob, or standing before Roman power, he did the same thing—he pleaded. He proclaimed the gospel and pressed for repentance—relentlessly.

Religious Liberty and Mission

Every Christian who cares about these issues of religious liberty and soul freedom needs to ask himself a serious question: *What is my mission?* This question matters because we're ministers of the gospel and not just nominal Christianity; the mission we are on does not begin after we attain religious liberty. The mission is what we are doing while we are appealing for religious liberty. We need to ask ourselves if we are pursuing freedom of conscience the way a prosecuting attorney would pursue it. That's not our mission. The devil is a prosecuting attorney. The devil understands how to condemn, destroy, and indict. That's not the Christian's endgame. The Bible has a much higher calling for us. We are ambassadors of reconciliation, criers pleading with those around us—just as though Christ Himself is physically shouting in the streets—"Be reconciled to God!"

If we need to know what that looks like, we can look at Paul. Does Paul sound like someone threatening Agrippa with a lawsuit? Or he's getting ready to unleash a verbal arsenal against his enemies? Of course not. Paul's message was not just a correction, it was an invitation. Is that us?

We must strive for this same kind of engagement, and here's why. There are people in our communities who see us as dangerous and oppressive because we believe that marriage is the union of one man and one woman. There are people in our communities who think we are insane because we believe that what they call an embryo or a fetus is their neighbor. There are people in our communities who believe that we are counterproductive by building churches in which black people and white people and Hispanic people love each other and are part of the same congregation. These many people in our neighborhoods and our cities and our culture don't understand what we're doing.

Our aim is not to vaporize them with well-crafted arguments. It is to speak the Word of truth. It is to call out unrighteousness and injustice wherever it is. But we don't stop there. We don't stop talking until we plead like Jesus pleads: "Come to me, all who labor and are heavy laden, and I will give you rest" (Matt. 11:28). That's our upshot, our clincher, our bottom line. That invitation won't stop all our arguments and it won't stop all our controversies. Sin is powerful; unbelief has a firm grip. The Lord told us that it often takes a long time for that Word to embed into the heart. But long or short, the Word is still the power of God for salvation. It has saved, it does save, and it will save.

The almost-gospel is tempting. Nominal Christianity can be appealing. The charm is in the ease. If the gospel is tame and Christianity generic, religious liberty is cheap and easy. But if we stand up and clearly say Jesus is King and isn't dead anymore, then the Pharisees and the Sadducees and the government will band together and oppose us. Our mission is to stand there with grace, mercy, and grit. Our mission is to speak with conviction, truthfulness, and kindness. Our mission is freedom and gospel with liberty and Jesus for all. If we find ourselves up against those who hate us, who misunderstand us, and even those who would like to put us in jail, may we refuse to look at them with balled-up fists. May we, like our brother Paul before us, look at them with teary eyes and preach to them with a bold tongue, and say: "Here is the Lamb of God, who takes away the sin of the world!"

Discussion Questions

1. Why is the freedom to believe so vital to the advance of the gospel?
2. What is the danger in making Christianity "generic" or "appealing" in our culture?
3. How does religious liberty relate to someone's salvation?

3

How Should the Christian Live?

Joe Carter

"DURING THE FIRST WORLD WAR," SAID THE ANTI-FASCIST politician Gaetano Salvemini, "we used to say that the situation in Germany was serious but not desperate, in Austria desperate but not serious, and in Italy desperate but normal."

Those of us concerned about religious liberty in America tend to have similar attitudes. Many are cautiously optimistic, and contend that while threats to religious freedom are serious, the situation is not desperate. Others consider themselves to be realistically pessimistic, believing that the issue is desperate but what we should consider "normal" in our secular society.

My own view is that we should take the Austrian approach: The state of religious liberty in America is desperate but not serious.

First, the bad news. The current threats to religious liberty are greater than they have been in a century, and are growing ever more ominous. If current trends prevail, the religious freedoms of Americans will soon become limited to the "freedom to worship." We will be allowed to worship however we choose in our heads, homes, and churches, but will be forbidden from acting on those beliefs in the public square. The situation is truly as desperate as it has ever been in America.

Now, the good news. The good news is that we have the Good News, the gospel of Jesus Christ. As Tim Keller explains,

> The "gospel" is the good news that through Christ
> the power of God's kingdom has entered history to
> renew the whole world. When we believe and rely on
> Jesus' work and record (rather than ours) for our rela-
> tionship to God, that kingdom power comes upon us
> and begins to work through us.
>
> Through the person and work of Jesus Christ,
> God fully accomplishes salvation for us, rescuing us
> from judgment for sin into fellowship with him, and

then restores the creation in which we can enjoy our
new life together with him forever.[5]

God's kingdom has entered history; the process of renewing
the whole world is now both inevitable and irreversible. No matter what happens, we know the ultimate victory belongs to Jesus.
That is why we can take a clear-eyed assessment of the threats to
religious liberty and conclude that the situation is desperate—
and yet, because our Lord reigns, we can stop the deterioration.

This is the tension that arises from the mystery of the
"already" and "not yet" Kingdom. The kingdom of God is present (Luke 17:20–21); the kingdom of God is not yet present
(Luke 19:11–12). Our job as Christians is to proclaim this Good
News, which is one of the primary reasons we must be defenders
of religious freedom. As Hugh Hewitt says,

> The effective and mass communication of the gospel
> depends on the freedom to proclaim it. Though it is
> possible to proclaim the gospel in the face of persecu-
> tion, the unfettered freedom to do so is much, much
> to be preferred. There are billions of souls who are
> up for eternal grabs, so the unfettered ability to reach
> them with the good news is a great and wonderful
> thing, hard to create and difficult to defend.[6]

Religious liberty is indeed hard to create and difficult
to defend. That is why many of us would prefer to remain

conscientious objectors in this latest front of the culture wars. But we don't have that luxury. We have been called to live and serve in a time and place when defending and protecting religious liberty is a duty of all believers.

While we may not all have the same role to play, each of us is called to partake of at least one of the following tasks:

- Identifying and predicting future threats related to religious freedom
- Working to roll back current restrictions on religious freedom
- Preventing further restrictions on religious freedom
- Protecting and defending those who are or will be affected by such restrictions

The goal of this chapter is to provide you with a few ideas for how to carry out these tasks over the next twenty to twenty-five years. A quarter of a century is both a long period in the life of an individual and a fleeting moment in the life of the church. It's just enough time to see the impending threats on the horizon and time enough to do something about them. But we must act now.

How to Predict the Future

Over the past fifty years, the rate of technological change and adoption has moved at an astoundingly rapid pace. It took forty-six years for electricity and thirty-five years for the telephone to be adopted by a quarter of American households. But it only took thirteen years for the cell phone and seven years for the Internet to reach the same levels within the population.

Ideas and concepts are also being adopted by society more quickly. Ideas that once seemed radical have gone from implausible to normal within less than a decade. The prime example—and one of the most significant threats to religious liberty—is the increasing acceptance of same-sex marriage. In 1996, 65 percent of Americans were opposed to same-sex marriage; in 2015, 61 percent *supported* same-sex marriage.[7] In May 2003, no states had approved gay unions; ten years later, one-fifth of the states allowed people to marry someone of the same sex. And now, same-sex marriage is legal in all fifty states.

How was the agenda to redefine marriage able to advance to the level of public policy? And how did it happen so quickly? To understand this seismic cultural shift, we should turn to an obscure, two-decades-old political theory.

To Move a Society, Move the Overton Window

The Overton Window, developed in the mid-1990s by the late Joseph P. Overton, describes a "window" in the range of public reactions to ideas in public discourse. Overton believed that the spectrum included all possible options in a window of opportunity:

> Imagine, if you will, a yardstick standing on end.
> On either end are the extreme policy actions for any
> political issue. Between the ends lie all gradations of
> policy from one extreme to the other. The yardstick
> represents the full political spectrum for a particular
> issue. The essence of the Overton window is that only
> a portion of this policy spectrum is within the realm
> of the politically possible at any time. Regardless of
> how vigorously a think tank or other group may cam-
> paign, only policy initiatives within this window of
> the politically possible will meet with success.[8]

All issues fall somewhere along this policy continuum, which can be roughly outlined as: Inconceivable, Radical, Acceptable, Popular, Policy. When the window moves or expands, ideas become more or less politically and culturally acceptable.

Overton's model was developed to explain adjustments in the political climate. But it can also help us to identify and classify the progress of various threats to religious liberty. Here, for example, is how the demonization of Christians opposed to same-sex marriage transitioned in four steps from Inconceivable to Policy:

Step #1: From Inconceivable to Radical. The first step requires having a person or group with some level of authority or legitimacy express a viewpoint that was once relegated to the political or cultural fringe. Consider, for example, the idea that Christians who refuse to use their artistic talents (such as photographers or bakers) for same-sex wedding celebrations would be considered bigots, the moral equivalent of the racial segregationists of the 1950s.

In 2006, many religious supporters of same-sex marriage considered this comparison to be, as Catholic law professor Doug Kmiec said, "inconceivable." Kmiec claimed that it would be inconceivable that "a successful analogy will be drawn in the public mind between irrational, and morally repugnant, racial discrimination and the rational, and at least morally debatable, differentiation of traditional and same-sex marriage."[9]

But the shift from Inconceivable to Radical had occurred long ago, at least as early as 1987. In an article for *Guide Magazine,* a pair of Harvard-educated homosexual-rights activists, Marshall Kirk and Hunter Madsen, wrote "The Overhauling of Straight America."[10] The two later expanded their argument and outline for homosexual normalization into a book, *After the Ball: How America Will Conquer Its Fear and Hatred of Gays in the 90's*, that was published by one of the America's largest publishing houses (Doubleday) and became a national best seller.[11]

In their essay, they propose the radical idea not only of portraying Christians as bigots, but also of using churches to carry out that mission:

> While public opinion is one primary source of mainstream values, religious authority is the other. When conservative churches condemn gays, there are only two things we can do to confound the homophobia of true believers. First, we can use talk to muddy the moral waters. This means publicizing support for gays by more moderate churches, raising theological objections of our own about conservative interpretations of biblical teachings, and exposing hatred and inconsistency. Second, we can undermine the moral authority of homophobic churches by portraying them as antiquated backwaters, badly out of step with the times and with the latest findings of psychology. Against the mighty pull of institutional Religion one must set the mightier draw of Science & Public Opinion (the shield and sword of that accursed "secular humanism"). Such an unholy alliance has worked well against churches before, on such topics as divorce and abortion. With enough open talk about the prevalence and acceptability of homosexuality, that alliance can work again here.

Step #2: From Radical to Acceptable. This shift includes redefinition or reconceptualization of a concept and the use of invective against those who refuse to accept the shift. For instance, the term *marriage* has been redefined to mean the state-endorsed copulation of any two (or possibly more) adults who want to share a bed and a tax form. Those who reject the shift from Radical to Acceptable are shamed into approving of the new redefining of terms and institutions by the deployment of a stingingly suitable insult, in this case, "bigot."

The application of the word *bigot* has become more effective than a billy club at beating people into submission on this issue. The insult is particularly effective when it comes from our fellow Christians. When the Kansas legislature passed a bill in 2014 protecting the religious freedom of businesses and individuals to refuse services to same-sex couples, Kirsten Powers, a Christian and columnist for *USA Today*, wrote that, "Christians backing this bill are essentially arguing for homosexual Jim Crow laws."[12]

For far too many Americans—including many Christians— there are few core beliefs they won't change to avoid being called a bigot. The disapproval of their Creator is unfortunate; enduring the disfavor of their peers is unimaginable.

Step #3: From Acceptable to Popular. This step merely requires personalizing the issue. In this particular case, the perception is created that the only reason any Christian would oppose homosexual behavior is not because of the clear teaching of Scripture but because of a lack of exposure to the LGBT community.

Christian ethicist David P. Gushee used this as an excuse not only to explain his own shift on the issue but also to argue that the church should change too:

> It is hard to describe exactly why my moral vision shifted in this way. But undoubtedly, it had much to do with my move to Atlanta in 2007 and my growing contact with LGBT people, especially fellow Christians. I hardly knew anyone who was gay before that move, but afterward, they seemed to be everywhere, and a few became very dear friends. It became clear to me—in a deeply spiritual place that I will allow no one to challenge—that God was sending LGBT people to me. The fact that one of these LGBT Christians is my dear youngest sister, Katey, has made this issue even more deeply personal for me than it would have been. The fact that one place where she developed a deep struggle with her sexuality was in evangelical churches has contributed to my new moral commitment to make evangelical families and churches safe places for LGBT people.[13]

Notice this is the same strategy Kirk and Madsen suggested in 1986: "This means publicizing support for gays by more moderate churches, raising theological objections of our own about conservative interpretations of biblical teachings, and exposing hatred and inconsistency." If an alternate interpretation is both possible and preferred, then any religious objections will automatically be deemed as rooted in animus and not a matter of which conscience should apply.

Step #4: From Popular to Policy. The shift from popular to "policy" (i.e., a position or policy preference protected by law) tends to happen rather rapidly. In some cases, though, policy doesn't catch up until the popular view is firmly embedded in culture. Consider the debates in 2014 and 2015 over Religious Freedom Restoration Acts.

The Religious Freedom Restoration Act (RFRA) is a federal law passed in 1993 to prevent other federal laws from substantially burdening a person's free exercise of religion. The legislation was introduced by Rep. Chuck Schumer (D-NY) on March 11, 1993, and passed by a unanimous U.S. House and a near unanimous U.S. Senate with three dissenting votes. The bill was signed into law by President Bill Clinton, who praised it as one of the greatest achievements of his presidency.

RFRA was intended to apply to all branches of government, and both to federal and state law. But in 1997 in the case of *City of Boerne v. Flores*, the Supreme Court ruled the RFRA exceeded federal power when applied to state laws. In response to this ruling, many individual states passed state-level Religious

Freedom Restoration Acts that apply to state governments and local municipalities.

As of 2015, twenty states have a Religious Freedom Restoration Act (AK, AL, CT, FL, ID, IN, IL, KS, KY, LA, MO, MS, NM, OK, PA, RI, SC, TN, TX, and VA). Ten other states have religious liberty protections that state courts have interpreted to provide a similar (strict scrutiny) level of protection (AK, MA, ME, MI, MN, MT, NC, OH, WA, and WI). With some exceptions (such as Mississippi), the state versions are almost exactly the same as the federal version.

None of the RFRAs even mention homosexuals, nor are they about discrimination. Yet when new RFRA legislation was introduced in 2014 and 2015, many media outlets identified the Indiana bill as being "anti-gay." Unfortunately, rather than being outraged at finding they were lied to by politicians and journalists, most Americans never bothered to learn the truth. Even Christians were duped into believing these were laws that moral people should oppose.

Neither the federal nor state RFRAs have ever protected a business that chose to discriminate against homosexuals. These laws have also never been used to protect a Christian who has appealed to religious conscience in refusing to serve same-sex weddings. But the misperception that the laws have the *potential* to be used in this way has led to a more broad-based opposition to legislation that protects religious freedom.

In retrospect, it's rather easy to connect the dots and show how same-sex marriage led to opposition of religious liberty. But while the Overton Window is a useful tool for allowing us to gauge how current threats to religious liberty have developed and to explain them to others, where it is most useful is helping us to identify and predict future threats.

In an interview on the science in science fiction, novelist William Gibson noted, "[T]he future is already here. It's just not evenly distributed yet." What Gibson meant was that the innovations in science fiction could already be found—at least in embryonic form—in our current ideas or technology. Much the same could be said about future societal and legal norms related to religious liberty: The threats are already here, they're just not evenly distributed yet.

Fortunately, the future is not causally closed, and if we can identify the threats that are "already here" we can work to prevent them from becoming more "evenly distributed" throughout society.

Working like Wilberforce

On May 22, 1787, Thomas Clarkson, William Wilberforce, and ten other British men formed a group known as the Committee for the Abolition of the Slave Trade. The committee was formed at a time when, as historians have estimated, the profits of the slave trade created up to one-in-twenty of every pound circulating in the British economy. The only thing more preposterous than their attempt to abolish slavery in Britain (and, subsequently, the world), was the speed with which they achieved their goal.

From a core of twelve men—a number intentionally patterned after the twelve disciples of Jesus—arose a popular movement that grew to include millions of people around the globe. The committee managed this remarkable feat by working tirelessly to create disciples at home and abroad who would help spread their message. Employing artists, writers, politicians, and apolitical housewives, the committee and its sympathizers created books, pamphlets, and works of visual arts to hammer home the horrors of slavery.

In pockets around the United Kingdom women held antislavery meetings in their parlors. In the United States, homegrown abolitionists and disciples of their forebears in Great Britain organized strong popular uprisings against the peculiar institution and practical acts of rebellion like the Underground Railroad. Masses of individuals, usually organized in small, dispersed clusters, distributed literature, engaged in debates, hosted political rallies, and cultivated the relationships necessary to convert others to the cause.

The efforts of these small groups proved to be a remarkable success. By the mid-1800s Britain abolished a five-thousand-year-old institution, and in less than one hundred years those small clusters of Christian men and women had fanned a small flame of hope into the roaring fire of nineteenth-century abolitionism, changing the world forever.

Christians aren't fatalists. We serve a living God who is sovereign over all creation. When faced with injustices, like slavery, we can commit to bold actions knowing that with the help of our God we can change the world. History has shown that the Lord can and will use dedicated Christians to close the Overton Window and reverse the shift from "policy" to "inconceivable." Just as William Wilberforce and his friends were able to shift on the British slave trade and evangelical abolitionists were successful in helping to end slavery in America, we can roll back some of the current restrictions on religious liberty.

Those who are motivated to be like Wilberforce and take direct action will develop their own strategies and tactics for advancing the cause. They don't need any more advice; they just need our support. Seek them out and find out how you can help them to be more effective.

Convictional Inaction

The Wilberforces of religious liberty are dedicated, indomitable, and tireless. In other words, they are engaged with this issue in a way that the average person in the pew will never be.

What is needed is a plan for those who are not likely to give much attention, energy, or time to this issue. We need a plan for this group that comprises the vast majority of believers.

Fortunately, we don't necessarily need Christians to march in the streets; we just need for our brothers and sisters in Christ to refuse to take the next step on the path to destruction. What we need from them is *convictional inaction.*

As it relates to religious freedom, convictional inaction is the mere refusal to side with the forces of anti-liberty. For example, if every Christian in America who truly cared about religious liberty refused to vote for any candidate—regardless of political party—who opposes laws protecting religious freedom, the restrictions would end within two election cycles. That's a nonpartisan approach that applies convictional inaction to solve the problem by literally doing nothing.

Similarly, if every Christian in America simply refused to condone the redefinition of marriage, we wouldn't have Christians being threatened by fines and bankruptcy for following their theologically informed consciences. If that sort of committed, convictional inaction—specifically a refusal to abandon Christian ethics—had already been in place, we could have prevented a lot of the problems we now face.

When properly applied, large-scale convictional inaction is one of the most powerful tools at our disposal.

Such convictional inaction, though, often requires as much courage as conviction. Unfortunately, for the past several decades America has produced an overwhelming number of Christians who are adept at explaining why they can support almost any issue that is antithetical to Christianity and depressingly few who can give reasons why we should adhere to the teachings of Scripture and the wisdom of the church. This is especially true when it comes to religious freedom.

To roll back current restrictions on conscience, we will need to educate our fellow believers about why religious freedom is important—and explain why we must defend religious liberty for people of all faiths. In addition, we will need to draw clear lines of distinction between what is and is not legitimately allowed by Scripture and encourage others to stand for the truth. Error in theology inevitably leads to erosion of religious conscience.

Personalize the Slippery Slope

While much of our focus should be on reversing current negative trends, we ought also to be continuously working to prevent further disintegration of our freedoms.

Christians with foresight could—and have—identified the steps in the Overton Window for almost every current challenge we now face. Too often, though, they are dismissed because they appear to be invoking a slippery slope argument (i.e., an idea or course of action that will lead to something unacceptable, wrong, or disastrous).

A slippery slope argument is merely a claim that "A will lead to B" either as an inevitability, as an increased probability, or as a logical outcome. Slippery slope arguments are often misunderstood, and many people mistakenly think their use is always logically fallacious. (As a general rule, if someone summarily dismisses a slippery slope claim, he or she is probably not the type of person who understands how arguments work. For instance, there are numerous legal precedents related to religious liberty where people have argued that accepting legal decision A will lead to B and have been proven correct.)

The problem with slippery slope arguments is not that they aren't legitimate or valid, for they certainly can be. The problem is they're generally rhetorically ineffective because many people either fail to think logically or are apathetic about the resulting consequences. One example of why appeals to the slippery slope are ineffective is summed up in Rod Dreher's "Law of Merited Impossibility":

> The Law of Merited Impossibility is a concept helping explain the paradoxical way elite opinion makers frame the discourse about the clash between religious liberty and gay civil rights. It is best summed up by the phrase, "It's a complete absurdity to believe that Christians will suffer a single thing from the

expansion of gay rights, and boy, do they deserve
what they're going to get."[14]

As Dreher's Law shows, the reason many people reject slippery slope arguments is that they support A *even if it leads to
B*—they just don't want to admit it yet. We see this frequently
in relation to religious liberty and same-sex marriage. Those who
used to claim that no one would ever be forced to serve same-sex
weddings are now calling for the state to force people to serve
same-sex weddings.

Logically speaking, this slippery slope outcome was never
really disputable. But many advocates of homosexual unions did
dispute it because it weakened their own position. Now that their
own position is gaining public acceptance, though, they are willing to now shrug and say, "So what if it *does* require Christians
to violate their conscience?"

Once we've slidden down the slippery slope, supporters of
the sexual revolution are often more willing to admit we were
right about what would happen, and they just aren't all that concerned about it. For people who were concerned, though, such an
admission comes too late.

When we identify the slippery slope—or a shift in the
Overton Window—we need to find a way to explain the connection to those who aren't yet convinced and are open-minded
enough to still consider the logical implications. One of the most
effective ways to do that is to make the arguments personal. As

Rachel Lu says, "If the public understands who you are and why you live in a particular way, they're usually willing to accommodate you to some extent. If not, they won't trouble to protect you against the incursions of the Progressive state."[15]

We are often provided examples by some where the mere exposure to homosexuals or transgendered individuals is enough to cause people to give up their deeply held religious views. Because it has been so effective for the other side, we should consider using it for our purposes too. Rather than making abstract claims about how some hypothetical person may be forced to violate their conscience, we need to provide flesh-and-blood exhibits to show the harm being done.

A particularly effective example has been Barronelle Stutzman, a grandmother and longtime florist, who was sued by the state of Washington for acting consistent with her Christian faith. As the Alliance Defending Freedom explains,

> Barronelle referred a longstanding customer to nearby florists because she could not in good conscience create custom arrangements and provide wedding support for his same-sex wedding. This ruling prevents Barronelle's case from going to trial and makes her personally responsible for paying any damages and attorney's fees incurred by the same-sex couple and the State of Washington. Everything she's worked to

build, including her home, her family business, and
her life savings are now at risk.[16]

Stutzman's gentle demeanor and commitment to following
Christ while serving others helped many Americans to better
grasp why it was wrong to force her to violate her conscience. She
is a model for how to personalize the slippery slope by putting a
human face on the cause.

To prevent further decline of religious freedom, we need
to learn to argue more effectively by learning to argue more
personally.

Be a Backstop for the Courageous

Stutzman's example also shows why it is imperative that
we find ways to protect and defend those whose religious liberties have been violated. Stutzman is incredibly brave and has
expressed a willingness to face the consequences of her convictions. She has also been fortunate to receive financial support by
those outraged by the injustice done to her. Because she is one
of the first to stand, Stutzman has been the recipient of much
generosity from her fellow Christians.

But Stutzman was the first; what will happen to the fourth,
fortieth, or four hundredth person who is affected by the same
law? Will we be there for them too?

What happens to the professor who loses tenure for professing her faith? What will become of the minister who refuses to let his church be used for a same-sex wedding? We can only expect people to stand firm when the church is standing with them. Individual acts of courage need to be backstopped by the communal support of the church.

The time to act on this is now, before the problem grows too large. We need to begin putting systems and programs in place to help those who will be affected by these restrictions in the near future. Some believers will need financial support to pay for the government fines. Others will need help finding a job when they are fired for holding firm to their faith. And in the future we may even have brothers and sisters who need someone to watch their children because they have been jailed for refusing to put Caesar before Christ.

The Persecution Trajectory

The idea that Christians may soon be jailed for their faith may sound absurd, like a scare tactic used on direct mail to solicit funds for a political cause. And it's true that *persecution* is a term that is used all too loosely in America. At a time when Christians are being killed for their faith in the Middle East it's absurd for believers in the U.S. to claim they are persecuted when someone says, "Happy Holidays," instead of, "Merry Christmas."

But if we are taking an honest assessment of the state of religious liberty in America, we must admit that true persecution in the future is a possibility. We are on a trajectory where persecution of faithful believers could be common by the end of the century.

In remarking on the problem of faith in our secular world, the Roman Catholic priest Cardinal Francis George said, "I expect to die in bed, my successor will die in prison, and his successor will die a martyr in the public square." In April 2015, Cardinal George died—in his bed. Like George, I expect that his successor—as well as many Baptist, Lutheran, and Presbyterian ministers—will die in prison. Where I disagree is with the time line and on which generation of successor the persecution will fall.

I believe we still have some time before George's prediction comes true. We even have time to prevent that outcome. The situation is indeed desperate, but we can prevent it from becoming serious.

Discussion Questions

. . . .

1. What current threats to religious liberty can be identified for each of the four steps of the Overton Window (e.g., Inconceivable to Radical; Radical to Acceptable; Acceptable to Popular; Popular to Policy)?

2. What individual or groups are "working like Wilberforce" to roll back some of the current restrictions on religious liberty? What practical steps can we take to aid them in their efforts?

3. What are four practical steps your group or church can take to provide communal support for Christians who will be directly affected by standing up for their religious convictions?

How Should the Church Engage?

Jennifer A. Marshall

IN THE SPRING OF 2015, A FIRESTORM OF PROTEST OVER A RELIGIOUS freedom law enacted in Indiana revealed something startling. Outrage focused not so much on the protection itself—it was an unremarkable policy already in place at the federal level and in nineteen other states—but on actions motivated by one particular belief that might be protected under the law. Perhaps the starkest example of such opposition appeared in an Easter Sunday op-ed titled "Bigotry, the Bible and the Lessons of Indiana," by *New York Times* columnist Frank Bruni:

> [O]ur debate about religious freedom should include
> a conversation about freeing religions and religious
> people from prejudices that they needn't cling to and
> can indeed jettison, much as they've jettisoned other
> aspects of their faith's history, rightly bowing to the
> enlightenments of modernity.[17]

The particular "prejudice" Bruni highlighted, and the focus of the controversy in Indiana, was orthodox religious teaching that homosexual relations are sinful and that Christians should not condone them. Bruni suggested that it was time to leave such beliefs on the ash heap of history, and he cited several religious denominations that have already done so.

Religious freedom controversies are no longer limited to friction over religious expression in the public square about, say, a Christmas crèche on a courthouse lawn or a student-led prayer at a public school graduation. Now critics raise questions about whether certain Christian convictions are incompatible with the common good.

This puts the controversy, unavoidably, at the heart of the church.

The future of religious liberty in the United States rests largely on churches' willingness to stand on the truth of God's Word, to equip Christians to speak and to act on that truth in their everyday lives, and to convey that we do so out of a desire for the good of all.

Stand on the Truth

To face these new religious liberty challenges, churches must correctly handle and actively teach the Word of God. Traditional biblical hermeneutics—the study of how to rightly understand Scripture—will be put to the test. In the same column mentioned above, Frank Bruni laid down the gauntlet: "There's a rapidly growing body of impressive, persuasive literature that looks at the very traditions and texts that inform many Christians' denunciation of same-sex relationships and demonstrates how easily those points of reference can be understood in a different way."[18] But biblical teaching about sexuality is not so easily interpreted away.

Beginning in the first two chapters of Genesis and throughout the Old and New Testaments, the Bible unequivocally teaches that human beings are created in the image of God, male and female, made for each other in marriage and community. Each element of that statement of belief about life and sexuality is increasingly challenged in culture and in law.

The Bible teaches that truth exists, and there is a created reality. Even if a legislature or court says otherwise, the created truth about marriage, the union of a man and a woman, will not change. Even if public policy asserts that gender is a social construct rather than a biological reality, it will not alter the truth of Genesis 1.

The Bible also testifies to a transcendent moral order: right and wrong rest in the unchanging character of God, not shifting standards. Majority opinion or congressional votes can't change that, however much they argue for relativism.

As Christians, we must speak and act in accord with scriptural truth, regardless of what the laws of the land may say, regardless of what pressure the majority may exert, and regardless of how much elite editorialists may condescend.

The consistency of Christian witness to the truth is critical to the future of religious liberty. We claim that our faith affects all of life, and opponents are eager to call our bluff if it does not. That much was clear when Christian nonprofit groups who challenged the health insurance mandate requiring coverage of abortion-inducing contraceptives faced scrutiny about the coherence of their pro-life ethic. The hostility toward Christian wedding service providers who decline to facilitate a same-sex ceremony shows critics' resistance to the comprehensive implications of the gospel for all of life. Threats and fines against such bakers, photographers, and florists aim to challenge the idea that faith has a place in the workplace.

One of the most pressing apologetic tasks in the twenty-first century, therefore, is to articulate how faith transforms the Christian individual, the church community, and groups gathered around the tenets of the faith. Churches need to shape members' consciousness of this distinctiveness and inform neighbors' understanding of it as well. We need better demonstrations and explanations of why faith makes a difference in the life of an individual or institution—and why the church is unlike any other human institution.

Some may read this appeal to defend embattled truths as an unnecessary distraction from the church's primary work of carrying out the Great Commission. But the "inconvenient truths" of the biblical worldview—the ones that are costly to defend in our culture today—cannot be neglected or denied in pursuit of evangelism or missions or justice. Seeking *shalom* means pursuing the flourishing of all our neighbors and our communities. We disserve our neighbors if we do not embrace and call others to embrace the truth about our nature and purpose as human beings. We cannot make disciples without explaining that following Christ means ordering our relationships and desires according to the truth of God's Word.

It is certainly possible to focus too much on one particular challenge or to treat one sort of sin, wrongly, as worse than others. But neglecting scriptural truths that an aching heart longs to hear is also a risk. The church needs passionate, creative leaders faithfully committed to the totality of God's Word who will grapple prayerfully with this tension in reaching a confused culture.

The Source and Scope of the Church's Liberty

Any church leader who speaks up on public issues like religious liberty will sooner or later have to deal with the challenge posed by the ubiquitous catchphrase "separation of church and state." The phrase is frequently misunderstood in public policy debates (because some use it to argue that religious voices and viewpoints have no place in politics). It's also particularly unhelpful as a starting point for churches considering their public witness. That's because "church-and-state" framing—whatever one interprets their "separation" to mean—refers merely to a legal relationship between two social institutions within our constitutional order. While that's an important concern, it's a completely inadequate framework for churches seeking to steward their role in public life.

Yet, because the church-state framework is so deeply ingrained in our thinking as American Christians, we may not even detect if it has displaced the biblical framework that ought to guide our approach to public life. That biblical framework transcends contemporary "church-state" categories. Long before today's conceptions of those institutional categories existed, God established His purposes in creation and in the plan of redemption, including His plan for the church. This reality, not human laws, provides the source and scope of the church's liberty.

Why does this matter? If we let popular ideas about the separation of church and state drive our thinking, then we are likely to adopt conventional concepts about the roles of the church and the state. We will be susceptible to the tides of a particular era, rather than subject to what God's Word teaches. Today, for example, increasingly expansive government disregards many aspects of human dignity and presumes authority to redefine even the Creation ordinance of marriage. From this vantage point, an encroaching state suggests a receding church.

From a biblical worldview, by contrast, government is responsible for a rather narrow range of a much broader human endeavor to order our lives together here on earth. Other social institutions like the family have a significant role to play as well. The church, as it serves the Creator and Lord who ordered and sustains the universe, has particular insights about ordering our lives together toward the good of all.

The purview of the church gets even larger when considering the gospel's social implications. The gospel announces the inauguration of a Kingdom that will surpass all earthly power, and the church is a manifestation of the earthly presence of God's kingdom in this time before its fulfillment. The church's social presence and posture toward government should testify to this now-and-not-yet reality and to its God-given liberty in public life.

From a biblical perspective, the God-ordained roles of the church and the government are distinct and complementary. Clearly the church must draw lines with regard to how far to extend its application of biblical teaching to the current civil context. The boundaries defining the church's appropriate engagement on any given topic of public life ought to be drawn *by the church*—not the government. The church should discern how to use its liberty for public witness according to theological criteria that take into account God's normative Word, the gravity of the particular situation, and how taking a public stance will affect the church's testimony to the gospel.

In thinking about such questions, some have been particularly concerned not to allow the mission Christ has given His church to be disrupted by political concerns. Diminishing the greatness of the gospel by constantly entangling churches in social concerns is a legitimate risk to be avoided. But for the church to remain silent on great moral and social questions of the day that are central to the gospel is to make God's lordship small.

Churches can speak to matters of civil concern on which biblical teaching is clear in a way doesn't compromise the church's charge to preach the gospel. To the contrary, some situations may require clear and public proclamations of biblical truth so the force of the gospel's witness is *not* compromised.

Church leaders should consider the exercise of its liberty in the public square case by case, committing themselves to prayer and using three criteria as a framework to discern when to speak out on specific issues of public life as the church: 1) the clarity of the Bible's normative standard on the issue; 2) the severity of the situational challenge to this truth; and 3) their responsibility to equip believers and to reach nonbelievers with a clear testimony to the lordship of Christ over all creation. The church as the church should speak specifically to public questions of direct, clear, and central biblical significance in which the church's witness to the gospel will be implicated.

For the Good of All

The laws of this land generally protect religious liberty so long as it does not disrupt the common good. So it is concerning to hear Christian views that dissent from popular or elite opinion be accused of harming the public good. In one example, Christian family-owned businesses and religious charities seeking relief from the coercion of the contraception insurance mandate were accused of waging a "war on women." A religious freedom policy allowing a day in court for a photographer whose convictions prevent her from using her God-given talents to promote a same-sex wedding was smeared as a "license to discriminate" against gays and lesbians.

Such accusations grossly distort Christian teaching and defy common sense. Tellingly, even some supporters of same-sex marriage see a problem with the coercion faced by an evangelical photographer in New Mexico who declined to photograph a lesbian commitment ceremony and was hauled before the state Human Rights Commission as a result. That shouldn't happen, writes one same-sex marriage advocate, and "gay photographers and bakers shouldn't be forced to work religious celebrations."[19] Freedom goes in both directions.

Whether a given pundit or lawmaker would make the same choice as the evangelical photographer is beside the point. A person does not need to have exactly the same scruples about birth control to agree with the Little Sisters of the Poor—a group of nuns caring for the elderly, who challenged the Obama administration's insurance mandate for contraceptive coverage—that they should not have to include such coverage in their employee health plan. Nor do all Americans have to concur with the evangelical employers who argue that covering ella and Plan-B—two of the FDA-approved contraceptives that can act to end the life of an embryo—is morally objectionable and that the government should not coerce them to be involved in providing such drugs.

Religious freedom allows just such differences of opinion. When Christians defend the freedom to speak and to act in both private and public life consistent with conscience, we do so in the interest of all. We don't have to share the particular conviction of the individual or group that wants to exercise such freedom to realize that we all share an interest in maintaining freedom of conscience and freedom of speech against coercive policies or cultural trends.

In recent years, many Christians seem to have accepted the secularist claim that to argue publicly from a point of view that can be traced back to the Bible is forcing one's religion on others. Secularists say that they offer the only genuinely neutral perspective. Christians should not accept this myth of neutrality. Everyone argues from fundamental beliefs, whether or not they acknowledge it. Secularists charge that taking a stand on issues like abortion or marriage is "imposing your morality" on others. If that's true, then they are guilty of their own charge. Every public policy makes moral judgments about what is good, from seat belt laws to environmental protection standards to the definition of marriage. Even voting is an exercise in expressing a worldview.

It is not self-interested to apply a Christian worldview to questions of public policy. It is simply serving our neighbor, by testifying to the way God has made the world. After all, we serve the God who defines the common good. The first cultural task God gave human beings was to order society and care for creation in a way that reflects his design for human flourishing.

Applying that charge in our American public policy context today—where we have the freedom to shape our laws through debate and elections—means seeking consensus that reflects that design. We use reason to persuade, recognizing that competing worldviews sometimes may cloud the capacity to reason together.

In spite of that, we can engage confidently on the basis of our beliefs with those who oppose us, appealing to their best interests and the longing we know that God has placed in the hearts of all human beings—a longing for the transcendent, for fulfillment, for wholeness (Eccl. 3:11).

Get Equipped

Congregations and religious ministries should anticipate conflicts based on their views that marriage is exclusively the union of a man and a woman and that sexual relations are properly reserved for marriage. It is important that pastors, church and ministry leaders, and Christian citizens be prepared to deal with such issues from a biblically informed perspective, having thought through what Scripture requires and what is negotiable in their specific context.

Church and ministry leaders should get acquainted with the kinds of challenges that are emerging and consider how it will impact their particular church or nonprofit organization. They should familiarize themselves with any state or local "non-discrimination" policy regarding sexual orientation or gender identity (SOGI). They should also learn what kind of religious liberty protections or exemptions might exist in state or local law.

Leaders should conduct an evaluation of their organization's internal policies that will be shaped by a biblical view concerning marriage and sexual relations. This will likely include, for example, organizational policies regarding employment standards, employee health and life insurance, facilities usage (including weddings), membership, and counseling (including marriage-related counseling).[20] A church or ministry should consider the scope of its programs, and its policies concerning all the categories of individuals involved. For example, a church-affiliated school should evaluate its policies expressing expectations for teachers, students, and parents.

Church or ministry leadership should take prudential steps now to shore up policy in the event of future legal challenge. Denominational leadership can provide assistance to individual congregations by establishing guidance for all participating entities. Whether at the denominational or congregational level, seeking formal legal counsel is prudent.

Churches should also prepare to help individual Christians with the kinds of decisions they will have to make in their daily callings. Churches have a pastoral duty to equip their members to stand on the truth in their everyday lives. That includes preparing individuals to speak and to act consistent with the biblical understanding of marriage and sexuality in their workplace. As the society around us grows increasingly hostile toward biblical views about marriage, sexual orientation, and gender identity, there will be conflicts across a wide range of professional situations. Individuals will need discernment in numerous vocations, from wedding-related services (photographers, bakers, florists, wedding planners) to teaching to social work to public office.

The case of counseling student Julea Ward offers an example of how such conflicts can arise in the context of the workplace. In March 2009, Julea was expelled from the graduate counseling program at Eastern Michigan University when she referred a client seeking counseling regarding a homosexual relationship. Because of her Christian faith, Julea did not want to provide counseling about sexual relationships outside of marriage (whether heterosexual or homosexual). She informed her practicum supervisor and was advised to refer the client, but then the school initiated a disciplinary process that resulted in her expulsion. The Alliance Defending Freedom represented Julea in a case that reached the Sixth Circuit Court of Appeals, which ruled in her favor, affirming her religious liberty. The university declined to appeal the case and a settlement was reached in December 2012—a vindication of Julea's religious freedom.

Christian education leaders in churches should seek out resources—or in the absence of appropriate materials, develop them—to assist individual Christians like Julea Ward in reasoning through the moral implications of particular workplace decisions. Individuals can also be equipped through Sunday school classes, support groups, mentoring, and counseling.

Policy Protection

Religious freedom protections in law should recognize the broad role of the church. Public policy must not hinder churches' God-given authority to proclaim the Word of God privately and publicly. Policy should not undermine the integration of faith in all aspects of a church or ministry. Nor should it prevent pastors and church leaders from taking public stands motivated by their faith.

In the fall of 2014, Houston Mayor Annise Parker actually attempted to do just that. After several local pastors led a petition drive to reverse a policy allowing individuals to use the bathroom of their gender identity choice rather than their biological sex, Parker tried to intimidate five of them by issuing subpoenas for their sermons and communications referencing the issue. But the mayor's overreach backfired and spread national outrage; the subpoenas were withdrawn.

Rightly understood, religious freedom should extend to individuals and to the variety of groups in which we come together, including churches, religious ministries, and family-owned businesses that seek to integrate faith and work. Church leaders should recognize the need to defend religious liberty not just for churches and for religious ministries, but also for individual Christians in their daily callings. They should be particularly wary of policies that might protect a church on Sunday but not its congregants Monday through Friday in the work world.

Christians should be on guard against efforts to reduce religious freedom to the mere freedom of worship, which have already appeared in several federal policies. "Freedom of worship" implies that religious faith is something to be contained within the four walls of a church or home. By contrast, a robust view of religious liberty protects the freedom to speak and to act on the basis of faith in both private and public, 24/7.

In the particularly challenging area of marriage and sexuality, specific religious liberty protections are necessary. Policy at the federal, state, and local level should protect the freedom of churches, other institutions, and individuals to speak and to act consistent with the truth that marriage is the union of a man and a woman, and that sexual relations are properly reserved for marriage. Laws should prohibit government from discriminating against individuals or groups who hold such views, in areas like tax policy, grants, contracts, accreditation, and licensing.

Promote Peace

The current feverish attacks on religious liberty broke out in the spring of 2014 in the state of Arizona. Minor clarifications to existing law got lost in an avalanche of gross mischaracterization as national pundits predicted the policy under consideration would usher in a "homosexual Jim Crow" regime with rampant denial of services by business owners to gays and lesbians.

The development was a stunning sign of increasing intolerance of basic protections for religious liberty. In reality, far from giving religious individuals or groups a "license to discriminate," the Arizona bill simply would have given religious entities that decline to participate in celebrating same-sex relationships an opportunity to have their day in court to argue for their religious freedom. This caricaturing of religious liberty in Arizona, Indiana, and elsewhere should be a wake-up call that prompts more Americans—particularly religious believers—to seek out the facts and to steward our freedoms more diligently.

Other cases have involved a backlash against simply participating in civil discourse about an important topic of public concern. In 2012, Angela McCaskill, associate provost for diversity and inclusion at Gallaudet, a federally chartered private university for the deaf in Washington, DC, was put on administrative leave after it became known that she had signed a petition—along with two hundred thousand other Maryland residents—to put a referendum on the ballot for citizens to review a same-sex marriage law passed by the state legislature. Mere participation in the political process was enough to warrant such treatment of McCaskill, the first black, deaf woman to earn a PhD from Gallaudet and a twenty-year veteran of the staff.

Similarly, the purge of Brendan Eich as Mozilla CEO in April 2014 stemmed from a furor over his donation six years earlier to the Proposition 8 campaign to define marriage as the union of a man and a woman in the California state constitution.

Such outrages can prompt despair, cynicism, and withdrawal. But they should not. These episodes should be catalysts to engage more vigorously and with greater perseverance in efforts to persuade through reason.

This pursuit of civil dialogue includes expecting and calling on all parties in a debate to use reason—not coercion or intimidation—to make their points as well. Failing to call out uncivil approaches shortchanges the dignity of those directly involved and of the surrounding community.

Media frequently portray these policy disputes as a zero-sum game. They need not be. Christians and other concerned citizens should be a part of seeking out the facts about the available policy and legal accommodations and working through the details in particular contexts to balance competing interests.

As we seek to faithfully interpret and apply God's Word in public life, we should heed the admonition of Romans 12:18 both in our method of engagement and in the proposals we recommend: "If possible, so far as it depends on you, live peaceably with all."

The Road Ahead

On the morning of April 25, 2015, the Supreme Court listened to oral arguments in cases challenging the freedom of states to make marriage policy reflecting the reality that it is the union of a man and a woman. Outside, groups supporting the truth about marriage called on the Court not to impose marriage redefinition on the country and instead to let debate continue. Many in the crowd held signs supporting religious liberty to send a message that redefining marriage would have consequences for such freedom, while advocates of same-sex marriage heckled the gathering.

Two months later, the Supreme Court imposed same-sex marriage on all fifty states. Since then, it has become even clearer that the costs of standing for biblical truth about marriage and sexuality will become increasingly costly. That should not be a cause for resignation—it is a call to act.

Churches must commit to prayer to face the religious liberty challenges ahead. Not only is cultural consensus on a number of questions concerning basic biblical truths about human dignity and sexuality eroding. Even the freedom to speak and to act consistent with biblical beliefs on these issues is threatened by pressures in culture and law. The twenty-first-century religious liberty challenge for churches in America is to stand firm on the truth, to equip individual believers to stand, and to make clear that the pursuit of religious liberty seeks the good of all.

Discussion Questions

1. Why is religious liberty so pivotal to the everyday workings of the local church?
2. How and why should Christians promote peace in society where serious disagreement exists on such matters as sexuality?
3. What biblical reasoning would you use to explain why believers should become active supporters for religious liberty? How would you support and equip them in that task?

What Does the Culture Say?

Hunter Baker

WHAT IS THE RELATIONSHIP BETWEEN A CULTURE AND THE idea of a constitutional right? Religious liberty is a value that explicitly rests upon the idea that religious ideas and practices exist that are not necessarily embraced by a majority of citizens. If a voting majority always existed to protect a particular religion or religious group, then there would be little need for a right designed to prevent a majority from overwhelming a minority. Religious liberty is the kind of principle we establish in our best and highest moments to defend against the things we might do when our passions are inflamed. Constitutional rights, then, are often countercultural in nature, especially when it comes to their application to specific cases.

Religious liberty is threatened today. It is threatened by our culture and by a sense of righteous anger directed against the beliefs of orthodox Christians. We need to speak to that culture and to encourage its members not to throw religious liberty away because they currently find it to be obnoxious or inconvenient relative to their desires.

I would like to begin examining the culture's attitude on religious liberty by discussing free speech. I start with that one because if there is anything we tend to think of abstractly as a nearly unquestioned constitutional right, it is free speech. Perhaps by looking at free speech for a moment, we can remind ourselves of the value of constitutional rights and set the stage for thinking again about religious liberty.

Why is free speech protected in the United States Constitution? Don't we all admire our commitment to free speech? Don't we see ourselves as being large-minded for protecting the marketplace of ideas come what may? If we are so devoted to the principle, then why the need for such a large protection as a constitutional right? Constitutional rights are different from other fences and hedges built into law. They can only be reversed with a massive, coordinated display of democratic force based on multiple, large majorities of citizens, states, and officeholders (or five of nine justices, but that is a matter for another day).

We protected free speech in our Constitution at the outset of the republic's life because we recognized that it is important to any real sense of citizenship and is a necessary part of being free. A person should be able to express ideas and have them heard by those who would choose to listen. A state that can limit speech is a state that can limit criticism of itself.

There is something interesting about free speech, though. While Americans would probably endorse a right to free speech in ultra-high numbers, those numbers predictably decline as we begin to reference particular situations. And that difference of support is not necessarily due to hypocrisy. A person who shouts "FIRE!" or "HE'S GOT A GUN!" in the crowded movie theater could cause a stampede resulting in deaths. A limitation on that kind of speech doesn't threaten the exchange of ideas or really impinge on expressive freedom. But what about a person who whips a crowd into a frenzy with highly charged remarks? Our tradition has included limiting that kind of speech, at least in so far as it strays into urging acts of violence. What if the speaker employs profanity? There have been times when a majority favored blocking that type of speech.

What if the speaker says something that many people find disagreeable or contrary to their own opinions? This is the real test. It is interesting to note that when the CEO of a well-known restaurant chain expressed his opinion that gay marriage is immoral and unbiblical, a couple of big city mayors immediately made intimidating comments suggesting that the restaurant chain was unwelcome in their respective cities.[21] Both mayors would surely endorse free speech, would wrap themselves in its mantle, and would attend fundraising banquets of organizations that purport to protect it. But the mountain of commitment for free speech crumbled almost instantly in the eyes of many in the face of a contrary opinion about something important.

Part of the value in framing a constitution, according to Thomas Aquinas, is that we might act more rationally and disinterestedly than we would in specific situations.[22] You can see the same logic at work with regard to the rules of a game. If we were to make up rules while the game is played, we might be tempted to make bad rules because of the outside influence of a particular moment or the people involved in that moment. Rules have to be made with cool heads. Constitutional rights such as free speech and, yes, religious liberty, are ideals chosen in isolation from the passions of a particular controversy. Thus, we determine to protect free speech before we know exactly what words will be spoken. Our resolve would likely waver otherwise.

Part of our constitutional logic, then, is in getting away from our interestedness in specific controversies because of the heat of our passions and our partisanship. We defeat it through abstraction of principles. We also insulate constitutional rights from the shifting sands of electoral majority. Political thinkers have virtually always been wary of the work of the demagogue and the mobs aroused by such persons. When we create a constitutional right, we say to ourselves in calm reflection that this is a thing that should be protected from shifts in our democratic mood. We can predict our emotions will shift just as we might predict we will want a piece of chocolate cake at just the wrong moment near midnight. In the making of a constitutional right, we insure ourselves against the appetites of democratic feeling. Part of the greatness of the United States is because our founding generation providentially threaded the needle in constructing a constitutional regime that provided the basis for ordered liberty. Our democratic republic operates on more than mass feeling or charismatic leadership. It constrains those things with a set of laws that are not easily changed.

I began this discussion with a focus on free speech because it is the part of the Bill of Rights that enjoys the best public relations. Few people would resist the idea that free speech is a critical part of the American order. To be American is to be able to freely and vigorously criticize the government with our voices, with our newspapers, with our blogs, with our social media, and with whatever new device comes to hand. But it is important to note that the Constitution deals with religious liberty before it addresses free speech. Some have referred to religious liberty as our first freedom because of its position in the text of the First Amendment to the Constitution.

What does the culture think about this first freedom? I have already delivered part of the verdict by describing the nature of a constitutional right with reference to free speech rather than religious liberty. Americans do not understand religious liberty in the same way they do free speech. We lionize free speech, but when we have thought about religious liberty it has been primarily through the example of the Pilgrims. While the history is complex, the lesson we take from the Pilgrims and early American religious disestablishment is that everyone should be able to attend the church of their choice (or not at all). In addition, no one should have to pay taxes to support a church. And that is not a small achievement. But religious freedom takes on a new importance as the reach of the state becomes more extensive.

It is no accident that religious liberty cases have become far more prevalent as the scope of the state has increased. As government has grown, conflicts between the free exercise of religion and the activities of the government have multiplied. Prior to the last few years, most cases revolved around the practices of minority religions. Thus, the court was asked to rule on Amish insistence that children be removed from formal education before high school so as to avoid excessive worldliness and to learn important skills.[23] In another famous case, a Seventh Day Adventist refused to work on her Sabbath day (Saturday) and therefore was refused unemployment benefits when she wouldn't take a job that entailed Saturday work.[24] Neither of these cases would have matured into ripe controversies before things such as mandatory schooling and unemployment benefits came into being. It is likely that the reason the courts stepped in to protect the rights of the Amish parents or of the Seventh Day Adventist is that in both cases the individuals involved were part of deep religious minorities. Such persons could not count on legislatures to stop and consider their needs when making laws.

Religious liberty stands on shakier ground than free speech. The free exercise of religion, which President Obama has chosen to refer to as freedom of worship (largely so as to limit the reach of religious liberty protections), is about action. Religion entails a way of life. It is more than singing and praying and gathering in fellowship halls. Religion stakes a claim on a person. Christianity (the religion I know best) demands that the believer live an integrated life. To have integrity is to integrate one's beliefs with one's actions.

In a time when government was more limited and less ambitious, the encumbrances of religion upon a person were far less likely to collide with the regulatory regime of the state. That situation has clearly changed. Government does more and more. It seeks to aggressively right wrongs and to encourage a set of behaviors *and* beliefs. This point might seem to be primarily an ideological one, perhaps a prescriptive complaint about the size of government. Instead, I am attempting to describe the situation. Governments are growing. As they grow, there will be more conflict with religion. We could express the relationship mathematically. There is a finite amount of public space. The state has taken possession of a greater portion.

Nevertheless, it is probably something more basic than state power that is decisive when we think about religious liberty and whether we value it. Religious liberty raises questions about who we are and how we live together. While the speaker of verbal challenges or the writer of manifestos confronts the social system through a series of publishing or speaking events, the integrated religious personality (a person under the lordship of Christ, for example) may go on living each day in defiance of supposedly settled rules. This defiance is not in words, but also in ways of life.

When the integrated person is part of some deep minority in American life making little effort at cultural engagement (such as the Amish), then the world system of state and commerce (which we mostly enjoy and find beneficial) can afford to benevolently make accommodation. In such a situation, there is little concern that the deviation from the norm would spread. But we are no longer arguing about religious liberty in terms of what may seem like religious boutiqueries. No more little sects. No more isolated, ruralized tribes.

Think of how most Americans approach issues of immigration. We want to see assimilation. We can tolerate a significant amount of difference in the short term, but we want assurance that the melting pot will continue to operate and that the foreign elements will become uniform. Today, that logic is mostly aimed at Mexicans, but in the past it pointed at Roman Catholics. Protestants feared that such persons owed allegiance to some old holy wizard halfway around the world rather than to Uncle Sam. Many described Catholicism as un-American and suited only for monarchical states or dictatorships. Some spread strange rumors about them. My mother (who grew up Catholic) was once asked if she would have to spend the first part of her wedding night with a priest. When John F. Kennedy ran for president in 1960, he essentially assured pastors in Houston that his Americanism was stronger than his Catholicism. There is an extent to which that attitude captures our culture's approach to religious liberty. Engage in your various deviations as long as it is clear what's on top. Or, if you won't subordinate, be small enough not to matter.

The challenge of religious liberty today is that those who seek to have their rights of conscience and free exercise recognized are part of a large demographic group. Both conservative evangelicals and serious Catholics have reservations about current legal initiatives such as the HHS Mandate and civil rights laws that deny a commercial right not to participate in a gay wedding if asked to do so. The problem, culturally speaking, is that those evangelicals and Catholics number in the tens of millions. Controversies regarding their rights don't collapse back into small communities. And they don't change simply because the times change. That is part of the problem from the perspective of the world system and the popular culture.

We are close to having a majority of Americans who view sexual orientation as a category that is roughly equivalent to race. They are certain that it is wrong to discriminate on race. Many are equally certain that it is wrong to discriminate on sexual orientation. They know that those who held retrograde opinions on race learned to change their attitudes or at least to keep their opinions hidden. It is probably the expectation of such persons that the more serious Christians will undergo a similar transformation. What they have failed to realize is that racism and segregation have nothing to do with Christianity. Those things were part of the social order and many Christians (especially in the South) mistook faithfulness to the civil cult for faithfulness to the church. Marriage, unlike race, is important to Christian belief. We believe that God made men and women for each other. There is clear warrant for that view both in Scripture and in nature.

Above, I referred to "a world system of state and commerce." It is powerful. And it desires sameness for the sake of efficiency. That world system is complemented by the civilizational cult.

Back in 2002, I traveled to Freiburg, Germany, with my wife and then six-month-old child to visit family members who were about to have a baby of their own. We were all together in a very small and cold walk-up apartment. I spent a lot of time during the days walking the streets of Freiburg just to deal with my claustro-phobic feelings. It was winter and the downtown area was beauti-ful. The central section of the town was a large circle. Little shops ringed the circle. In the middle of the circle was an enormous cathedral several centuries old. It was a marvel. With the snow falling I could imagine standing in the same spot centuries ago around the time of Christmas. In my mind's eye I could see crowds of people walking into the area on its cobblestone streets to worship on Christmas Eve. This was the church as the center of a culture.

In the time of European Christendom, the Christian reli-gion served as the religion of the people and nations. Christian churches provided the official structure of worship and values in a community. It was the cult in the culture. The culture always has a cult.

For a period of centuries, the Christian faith operated in tandem with the mass cult. The pioneering sociologist Emile Durkheim viewed religion as something like society worshipping itself. At various points, devout Christians rebelled at the com-promises required of being tied to the community cult and thus you had a Francis, a Tyndale, a Luther, or a Great Awakening. One might argue that we have been unraveling the interwoven fabric of Christianity and the community cult since that time, but faster in the last half century.

In America today, the antithesis between church and cul-ture has become fairly clear. Christianity does not provide the "cult" in the culture. The American religion can be found in the earnest professions of movie stars, media personalities, ambitious politicians, and corporate executives. The new American religion, while shaped by Christian ideas about the dignity of human beings and Christian benevolence, is increasingly intolerant of Christian orthodoxy. We have seen a major corporation fire one of its founders who was the CEO for having donated to a traditional marriage referendum in California. The mere act of his previously unpublicized donation was enough to establish his unsuitability, his out-of-stepness with the new American faith. He had become, in fact, a type of heretic. In recent times, we have seen the mayor of Atlanta terminate his fire chief because of his expression of traditional Christian sexual morality in a book written for his Sunday school class. There is a sense in which holding ordinary Christian beliefs is now a form of cultural heresy marking one as unfit for a position of authority.

Whether the issue is the HHS Mandate regarding the provision of contraceptive products or new attitudes regarding same-sex romance and marriage, the group representing the theology of this new Durkheimian cult has demonstrated a willingness to push those who disagree into conforming. The Christian florist or baker with objections to working on a gay wedding must be brought to heel. There is forgiveness offered by the new faith. One may hope for a chance to attend sensitivity training so as to avoid a ruinous fine. When the U.S. Supreme Court handed down a narrow decision in favor of Hobby Lobby despite its heretical view of biological ethics, the members of the new community cult howled as though some peasant had failed to remove his hat in the presence of the king. The dangerous Christian sect had been granted a stay.

The situation forces us to be honest about where we are as the church. Fortunately, we have prior history to guide us. If you look at the history of the church in the West, it has really operated on two models: the *comprehensive* church and the *regenerate* church. If you think about the picture I painted of the church at the center of the city in Freiburg, and my thoughts about what it might have been like at the height of European Christendom, then you have a sense of the comprehensive church. The comprehensive church was tightly interwoven with the political and legal structures. To be born into the community was effectively to be baptized as well. We still see little vestiges of the comprehensive church in Europe, but the lesson seems to be that legal establishment ultimately saps the church and leaves it subsidized and conforming.

In the United States, we had formal disestablishment early on in our history, but we continued on with an informal establishment for more than a hundred years after that. Even if we look back to the Eisenhower years of the 1950s, you could find strong encouragement generally to "attend the church of your choice," which really amounted to a strong nod in favor of the Judeo-Christian mix of Protestants, Catholics, and Jews. President Eisenhower laid the cornerstone of the National Council of Churches building (sometimes called "the Godbox") in New York City. During the time of informal establishment, Christians did not really need protections for their religious liberty. There was not much in the culture that wanted to impose itself on the faith. The culture still corresponded in significant ways with Christianity, even if somewhat subconsciously.

The Christian church of America today is not comprehensive in either the formal or informal senses. We, as evangelicals, have played a part in that development. We have made it clear that we desire no weak, watered-down, pink lemonade for blood sort of cultural religion. In this age, there is virtually no chance that we will again be Christians in the comprehensive mode. We will instead be like the early Christians in the sense that will be the regenerate church rather than the comprehensive church. The regenerate church has a membership based on conviction as opposed to one centered on assumed beliefs, geography, citizenship, and social power.

There will be many who will say, "Hallejujah! May it ever be so. The worst thing that ever happened for the church was Constantine's conversion!" And I understand that sentiment, although I give it two cheers rather than three. My reservation has to do with the fact that Constantine's conversion was a spectacular deliverance for the church of the time and arguably set the stage for the Christianization of Europe and the West.

The regenerate church has a sincerity and a spiritual power often lacking in the comprehensive version. But the regenerate church stands more at odds with the communities in which it exists. When the regenerate church criticizes "the world" and "worldliness," there are many who recognize themselves in the critique and do not care to hear it. The result is that the church moves from the center of things to more of an outside, challenging kind of position. That is no cause for panic. A Bible-reading people should not be rattled by it. We have some expectation of being on the outside if we are faithful.

Nevertheless, even if we are increasingly on the outside in the United States (and in the West, generally), the question of religious liberty remains. We have a rich genetic heritage of religious liberty in America. In our best moments, our nation dealt with religious dissent and variation through the logic of accommodation. The Amish children did not have to continue to high school. The Seventh Day Adventist did not have to agree to work Saturdays or lose eligibility for unemployment benefits. Rather than simply impose the blunt force of state power, we asked whether there might be some other way to respect the religious scruples of citizens. The relevant laws remained in force. Meanwhile, the states in question accommodated sincerely held religious beliefs that imperiled neither the health nor peace of the community.

By way of conclusion in discussing the way the culture thinks about religious liberty, I present two scenarios:

Scenario #1

Two men walk into a bakery. The owner of the bakery, who runs the small shop by herself with some part-time help, comes to the counter.

Bakery owner: Hello, how are you doing? May I help you?

Man #1: Yes, we're getting married and would like to order a wedding cake.

Bakery owner: Oh, I'm so sorry. I would love to make you a cake for almost any other occasion, but I am a Christian and do not wish to participate in a same-sex wedding. I know you disagree with me, but I feel that weddings are religious in nature and I would be uncomfortable being part of your nuptials. I know that creates some unpleasantness between us. I regret that.

Man #1: You are right. I disagree, but I understand your point of view. It is unlikely that I will do business with this shop again. Many of our friends in the gay community will not want to purchase from your store.

Bakery owner: Yes, I am sure that is true. I don't feel I can compromise on this point, but I would happily help you in any other way I can. Thank you for coming by. And thank you for respecting my feelings about the issue even if we don't agree.

Scenario #2

Two men walk into a bakery. The owner of the bakery, who runs the small shop by herself with some part-time help, comes to the counter.

Bakery owner: Hello, how are you doing? May I help you?

Man #1: Yes, we're getting married and would like to order a wedding cake.

Bakery owner: Oh, I'm so sorry. I would love to make you a cake for almost any other occasion, but I am a Christian and do not wish to participate in a same-sex wedding. I know you disagree with me, but I feel that weddings are religious in nature and I would be uncomfortable being part of your nuptials. I know that creates some unpleasantness between us. I regret that.

Man #1: Oh, you'll regret it all right. The civil rights laws of this state are applicable to commercial transactions such as buying wedding cakes. By not making a cake for our wedding, you will be in violation of those laws. I shall report you to the authorities. I may also initiate a lawsuit in which I will seek damages.

What does the culture think about religious liberty? If we go in the direction we're going, which is the direction of the world system and the new American civil cult, then the result will be like the second scenario above. Religion will have to be fully privatized and only lived out when the system cult toler-ates it. But if we think of religious liberty in the same way we do free speech, which is an important limitation on government and a support for freedom, then we will resist the system cult. The decision is being made right now, in the period in which we live. We have to hope that the culture will see the potential for a great loss of freedom as we move to a secularized version of the old Catholic proposal that "error has no rights." But I am not hopeful, because we are not thinking abstractly and passions have been stirred. May God preserve our liberty, but if that is not what He wills, then may He use this time to strengthen the church and to refine its love.

Discussion Questions

1. Why do you think the stability of law is important in providing for and protecting religious liberty?
2. What are the strengths of a "comprehensive" church in culture? What are the strengths of a "regenerate" church in culture?
3. Why is silencing different viewpoints harmful to society?
4. What is the difference between "religious freedom" and "freedom to worship"?
5. Why is the freedom of speech so closely related to religious freedom?

ADDITIONAL READING

Onward: How to Engage the Culture without Losing the Gospel by Russell Moore

Truth Overruled: The Future of Marriage and Religious Liberty by Ryan T. Anderson

God of Liberty: A Religious History of the American Revolution by Thomas Kidd

Religious Freedom: Why Now? Defending an Embattled Human Right by Timothy Shah and Matthew Franck

Conscience and Its Enemies: Confronting the Dogmas of Liberal Secularism by Robert P. George

Religious Liberty in the American Republic by Gerard Bradley

First Freedom: The Baptist Perspective on Religious Liberty edited by Thomas White and Jason G. Duesing

Clash of Orthodoxies: Law, Religion, and Morality in Crisis by Robert P. George

Free to Serve: Protecting the Religious Freedom of Faith-Based Organizations by Steven Monsma and Stanley Carlson-Thies

World of Faith and Freedom: Why International Religious Liberty Is Vital to American National Security by Thomas Farr

ACKNOWLEDGMENTS

TO THE MANY HANDS INSIDE AND OUTSIDE THE ERLC, WE thank you for your help and assistance on this book. The ERLC team provided joyful encouragement in the planning and execution of this series, and without them, it would never have gotten off the ground. We want to also personally thank Phillip Bethancourt who was a major visionary behind this project. We'd also like to thank Jennifer Lyell and Devin Maddox at B&H, our publisher, for their work in guiding us through this process.

ABOUT THE ERLC

THE ERLC IS DEDICATED TO ENGAGING THE CULTURE WITH the gospel of Jesus Christ and speaking to issues in the public square for the protection of religious liberty and human flourishing. Our vision can be summed up in three words: kingdom, culture, and mission.

Since its inception, the ERLC has been defined around a holistic vision of the kingdom of God, leading the culture to change within the church itself and then as the church addresses the world. The ERLC has offices in Washington, DC, and Nashville, Tennessee.

ABOUT THE CONTRIBUTORS

Hunter Baker J.D., PhD serves as university fellow for Religious Liberty at Union University. He is the author of three books on religion and politics and is a research fellow with the Research Institute of the Ethics and Religious Liberty Commission.

Joe Carter is senior editor at the Acton Institute, a communications specialist for the Ethics & Religious Liberty Commission of the Southern Baptist Convention, an editor for The Gospel Coalition, and an adjunct professor of journalism at Patrick Henry College.

Jennifer A. Marshall is vice president of the Institute for Family, Community, and Opportunity at The Heritage Foundation and senior research fellow at the Institute of Theology and Public Life at Reformed Theological Seminary in Washington, DC.

Russell Moore is president of the Ethics & Religious Liberty Commission of the Southern Baptist Convention.

Andrew T. Walker serves as director of Policy Studies at the Ethics & Religious Liberty Commission.

NOTES

1. James Madison, "Memorial and Remonstrance against Religious Assessments," http://press-pubs.uchicago.edu/founders/documents/amendI_religions43.html.

2. Quoted in Robert P. George, "What Is Religious Freedom?" *Public Discourse*, July 24, 2013, http://www.thepublicdiscourse.com/2013/07/10622.

3. Christian Smith, *Moral, Believing Animals: Human Personhood and Culture*, 1st ed. (New York; Oxford: Oxford University Press, 2009).

4. Madison, "Memorial and Remonstrance."

5. Tim Keller, "Gospel Definitions: Tim Keller," The Gospel Coalition. Accessed from http://www.thegospelcoalition.org/blogs/trevinwax/2008/03/07/gospel-definitions-tim-keller on April 1, 2015.

6. Hugh Hewitt, *A Guide to Christian Ambition* (Nashville, TN: Nelson Books, 2003), vii.

7. Pew Research Center, "Growing Public Support for Same-Sex Marriage." Accessed from http://www.people-press.org/2012/02/07/growing-public-support-for-same-sex-marriage/ on April 1, 2015; *Washington Post*, "Post-ABC poll - over 6 in 10 support gay marriage." Accessed from http://www.washingtonpost.com/page/2010-2019/WashingtonPost/2015/04/23/National-Politics/Polling/release_395.xml on April 1, 2015.

8. Nathan J. Russell, "An Introduction to the Overton Window of Political Possibilities," Mackinac Center for Public Policy. Accessed from http://www.mackinac.org/7504 on April 1, 2015.

9. Maggie Gallagher, "Banned in Boston," CatholicCulture.org. Accessed from http://www.catholicculture.org/culture/library/view.cfm?recnum=6935 on April 1, 2015.

10. Marshall Kirk and Hunter Madsen (a.k.a. Erastes Pill), "The Overhauling of Straight America." Accessed from http://library.gayhomeland.org/0018/EN/EN_Overhauling_Straight.htm on April 1, 2015.

11. Kirk and Madsen, *After the Ball: How America Will Conquer Its Fear and Hatred of Gays in the 90's* (New York: Doubleday, 1989).

12. Kirsten Powers, "Jim Crow Laws for Gays and Lesbians?" Accessed from http://www.usatoday.com/story/opinion/2014/02/18/gays-lesbians-kansas-bill-religious-freedom-christians-column/5588643 on April 1, 2015.

13. David P. Gushee, "I'm an Evangelical Minister. I Now Support the LGBT Community—and the Church Should, Too," *Washington Post*. Accessed from http://www.washingtonpost.com/posteverything/wp/2014/11/04/im-an-evangelical-minister-i-now-support-the-lgbt-community-and-the-church-should-too on April 1, 2015.

14. Rod Dreher, "The Law of Merited Impossibility," *The American Conservative*. Accessed from http://www.theamericanconservative.com/dreher/the-law-of-merited-impossibility on April 1, 2015.

15. Rachel Lu, "How to Save Religious Freedom," *The Federalist*. Accessed from http://thefederalist.com/2015/04/08/how-to-save-religious-freedom on April 26, 2015.

16. Alliance Defending Freedom, "The Story of Barronelle Stutzman." Accessed from https://alliancedefendingfreedom.org/arlene-flowers?referral=I0215ARLF1 on April 26, 2015.

17. See http://www.nytimes.com/2015/04/05/opinion/sunday/frank-bruni-same-sex-sinners.html?_r=0.

18. Ibid.

19. See http://www.cato.org/blog/marriage-equality-religious-liberty-freedom-association.

20. For further information, see Eric N. Kniffin, "Protecting Your Right to Serve: How Religious Ministries Can Meet New Challenges without Changing Their Witness," Special Report #177, November 9, 2015, http://www.heritage.org/research/reports/2015/11/protecting-your-right-to-serve-how-religious-ministries-can-meet-new-challenges-without-changing-their-witness.

21. Here, I am referencing the Chick-fil-A controversy of a few years ago and the reactions of the mayors of Chicago and Boston, respectively.

22. Thomas Aquinas, *Summa Theologiae*, Question 95, First Article. (I use this uniform method of citation for Aquinas because the book has been reprinted so frequently by so many different publishers.)

23. *Wisconsin v. Yoder*, 406 U.S. 205 (1972).

24. *Sherbert v. Verner*, 374 U.S. 398 (1963).